140 Prostate Cancer Juice, Salad, and Meal Recipes

The Cancer-Fighting Cookbook to a Better Life

By

Joe Correa CSN

COPYRIGHT

© 2019 Live Stronger Faster Inc.

All rights reserved

Reproduction or translation of any part of this work beyond that permitted by section 107 or 108 of the 1976 United States Copyright Act without the permission of the copyright owner is unlawful.

This publication is designed to provide accurate and authoritative information in regard to the subject matter covered. It is sold with the understanding that neither the author nor the publisher is engaged in rendering medical advice. If medical advice or assistance is needed, consult with a doctor. This book is considered a guide and should not be used in any way detrimental to your health. Consult with a physician before starting this nutritional plan to make sure it's right for you.

ACKNOWLEDGEMENTS

This book is dedicated to my friends and family that have had mild or serious illnesses so that you may find a solution and make the necessary changes in your life.

140 Prostate Cancer Juice, Salad, and Meal Recipes

The Cancer-Fighting Cookbook to a Better Life

By

Joe Correa CSN

CONTENTS

Copyright

Acknowledgements

About The Author

Introduction

Commitment

140 Prostate Cancer Juice, Salad, and Meal Recipes: The Cancer-Fighting Cookbook to a Better Life

Additional Titles from This Author

ABOUT THE AUTHOR

After years of Research, I honestly believe in the positive effects that proper nutrition can have over the body and mind. My knowledge and experience has helped me live healthier throughout the years and which I have shared with family and friends. The more you know about eating and drinking healthier, the sooner you will want to change your life and eating habits.

Nutrition is a key part in the process of being healthy and living longer so get started today. The first step is the most important and the most significant.

INTRODUCTION

140 Prostate Cancer Juice, Salad, and Meal Recipes: The Cancer-Fighting Cookbook to a Better Life

By Joe Correa CSN

There are certain factors that highly increase the risk of prostate cancer. The first, and most important of all, is definitely age. The risk of getting this type of cancer highly increases with your age. Another important risk factor is also your family history. If members of your family have had prostate cancer, you're more likely to develop it as well. Finally, obesity is the last but not the least risk factor you have to keep in mind. Overweight men are more likely to develop aggressive types of prostate cancer which are more difficult to treat.

The most common symptoms of prostate problems and cancer include urination abnormalities, pain, painful ejaculation, pelvic or abdominal pain, erectile dysfunction, extremity swelling, and blood in urine or semen. Although not all of these symptoms indicate prostate cancer, they might be a sign of some serious medical conditions that require an immediate medical intervention. Prostate cancer can only be diagnosed by tissue biopsy.

The question is what can you do to prevent prostate cancer? The answer lies in a proper diet. Our body is a truly fantastic organism that has the ability to defend and cure itself. This is why it's crucial to help your immune system to get stronger and boost your overall health.

These juice, salad, and meal recipes are a smart way to improve your health and help you prevent prostate cancer. Get started reading this book and see the difference it will make on your body.

COMMITMENT

In order to improve my condition, I *(your name)*, commit to eating more of these foods on a daily basis and to exercise at least 30 minutes daily:

- Berries (especially blueberries), peaches, cherries, apples, apricots, oranges, lemon juice, grapefruit, tangerines, mandarins, pears, etc.
- Broccoli, spinach, collard greens, sweet potatoes, avocado, artichoke, baby corn, carrots, celery, cauliflower, onions, etc.
- Whole grains, steel-cut oats, oatmeal, quinoa, barley, etc.
- Black beans, red bean beans, garbanzo beans, lentils, etc.
- Nuts and seeds including: walnuts, cashews, flaxseeds, sesame seeds, etc.
- Fish
- 8 – 10 glasses of water

Sign here

X_____

140 PROSTATE CANCER JUICE, SALAD, AND MEAL RECIPES: THE CANCER-FIGHTING COOKBOOK TO A BETTER LIFE

JUICE RECIPES

1. **Tomato Beet Juice**

Ingredients:

4 cherry tomatoes, halved

2 whole beets, sliced

1 cup of watercress, torn

1 rosemary sprig

1 oz of water

Preparation:

Wash the tomatoes and remove the stems. Cut each in half and set aside.

Wash and trim off the beets. Cut the green parts and cut into thin slices. Set aside.

Place the watercress in a colander and wash under cold water. Torn with hands and set aside.

Now, combine tomatoes, beets, watercress, and rosemary in a juicer. Process until well juiced. Transfer to a serving glass and stir in the water. You can add some salt if you like, but it's optional.

Refrigerate for 10 minutes before serving.

Nutritional information per serving: Kcal: 63, Protein: 4.1g, Carbs: 18.7g, Fats: 0.4g

2. Carrot Celery Juice

Ingredients:

1 large carrot, sliced

1 large celery, chopped

1 cup of fresh kale, chopped

1 small Granny Smith's apple, cored

1 tbsp of liquid honey

Preparation:

Wash and peel the carrot. Cut into thin slices and set aside.

Wash the celery and cut into bite-sized pieces. Set aside.

Rinse the kale under cold running water using a colander. Slightly drain and torn with hands. Set aside.

Wash the apple and cut lengthwise in half. Remove the core and cut into bite-sized pieces. Set aside.

Now, combine carrot, celery, kale, and apple in a juicer and process until juiced. Transfer to a serving glass and stir in the honey.

Add some ice and serve immediately.

Nutritional information per serving: Kcal: 179, Protein: 4.6g, Carbs: 34.3g, Fats: 1.1g

3. Asparagus Grapefruit Juice

Ingredients:

1 cup of asparagus, trimmed and chopped

1 whole grapefruit, peeled

1 whole lime, peeled

1 whole leek, chopped

1 oz of water

Preparation:

Wash the asparagus and trim off the woody ends. Chop into small pieces and set aside.

Peel the grapefruit and divide into wedges. Cut each wedge in half and set aside.

Peel the lime and cut lengthwise in half. Set aside.

Wash the leek and cut into bite-sized pieces. Set aside.

Now, combine asparagus, grapefruit, lime, and leek in a juicer and process until well juiced. Transfer to a serving glass and stir in the water.

Add some honey if you like, but it's optional.

Refrigerate for 10 minutes before serving.

Enjoy!

Nutritional information per serving: Kcal: 161, Protein: 6.3g, Carbs: 47.7g, Fats: 0.8g

4. Dandelion Juice

Ingredients:

1 cup of fresh dandelion greens, torn

2 medium-sized celery stalks, chopped

1 whole lemon, peeled

1 small Granny Smith's apple, cored

1 cup of cucumber, sliced

Preparation:

Wash dandelion greens thoroughly and torn with hands into small pieces. Set aside.

Wash the celery and cut into bite-sized pieces. Set aside.

Peel the lemon and cut lengthwise in half. Set aside.

Wash the apple and cut in half. Remove the core and cut into bite-sized pieces. Set aside.

Wash the cucumber and cut into thin slices. Fill the measuring cup and reserve the rest for later.

Now, combine dandelions, celery, lemon, apple, and cucumber in a juicer and process until juiced.

Transfer to a serving glass and add some crushed ice before serving.

Nutritional information per serving: Kcal: 97, Protein: 2.9g, Carbs: 29.7g, Fats: 0.7g

5. Broccoli Banana Juice

Ingredients:

1 cup of broccoli, chopped

1 large banana, sliced

1 small green apple, cored

1 small ginger knob, peeled

1 tbsp of liquid honey

Preparation:

Wash the broccoli and trim off the outer layers. Cut into small pieces and fill the measuring cup. Reserve the rest for later.

Peel the banana and cut into small slices. Set aside.

Wash the apple and cut in half. Remove the core and cut into bite-sized pieces. Set aside.

Peel the ginger knob and set aside.

Now, combine broccoli, banana, apple, and ginger in a juicer and process until well juiced. Transfer to a serving glass and stir in the honey.

Refrigerate for 10 minutes before serving.

Nutritional information per serving: Kcal: 261, Protein: 4.8g, Carbs: 57.7g, Fats: 1.1g

6. Green Tea Juice

Ingredients:

1 tsp of green tea

2 tbsp of hot water

2 whole kiwis, peeled

1 medium-sized pear, chopped

1 cup of fresh spinach, torn

1 cup of fresh mint, roughly chopped

1 whole lime, peeled

Preparation:

Combine green tea and hot water in a small bowl. Stir well and set aside to soak for 3 minutes.

Peel the kiwis and cut lengthwise in half. Set aside.

Wash the pear and remove the core. Cut into bite-sized pieces and set aside.

Wash the spinach under cold running water using a colander. Torn with hands and set aside.

Wash the mint and roughly chop it. Fill the measuring cup

and reserve the rest for later.

Peel the lime and cut lengthwise in half. Set aside.

Now, combine green tea mixture, kiwis, pear, spinach, mint, and lime in a juicer and process until juiced. Transfer to a serving glass and add some ice before serving.

Enjoy!

Nutritional information per serving: Kcal: 195, Protein: 9.4g, Carbs: 62.4g, Fats: 2.1g

7. Pomegranate Asparagus Juice

Ingredients:

1 cup of pomegranate seeds

1 cup of fresh asparagus, trimmed and chopped

1 whole lemon, peeled

1 tbsp of liquid honey

1 oz of water

Preparation:

Cut the top of the pomegranate fruit using a sharp paring knife. Slice down to each of the white membranes inside of the fruit. Pop the seeds into a measuring cup and set aside.

Wash the asparagus and trim off the woody ends. Cut into bite-sized pieces and set aside.

Peel the lemon and cut into quarters. Set aside.

Now, combine pomegranate seeds, asparagus, and lemon in a juicer and process until well juiced. Transfer to a serving glass and stir in the honey and water.

Add some ice and enjoy!

Nutritional information per serving: Kcal: 145, Protein: 5.1g, Carbs: 26.8g, Fats: 1.3g

8. Spinach Tomato Juice

Ingredients:

1 cup of fresh spinach, chopped

6 cherry tomatoes, halved

1 cup of cucumber, sliced

1 small ginger knob, peeled

¼ tsp of salt

Preparation:

Wash the spinach thoroughly under cold running water. Slightly drain and chop into small pieces. Set aside.

Wash the cherry tomatoes and remove the stems. Cut each tomato in half and set aside.

Wash the cucumber and cut into thin slices. Fill the measuring cup and reserve the rest for later.

Now, combine spinach, tomatoes, cucumber, and ginger in a juicer and process until juiced. Transfer to a serving glass and stir in the salt.

Serve immediately.

Nutritional information per serving: Kcal: 52, Protein: 7.4g, Carbs: 14.5g, Fats: 1.1g

9. Watermelon Blueberry Juice

Ingredients:

1 cup of watermelon, cubed

2 cups of blueberries

1 whole lime, peeled

1 cup of fresh basil, torn

¼ tsp of cayenne pepper, ground

1 oz of water

Preparation:

Cut one large watermelon wedge. Using a sharp paring knife, peel and cut into small cubes. Remove the seeds and set aside.

Place the blueberries in a large colander. Rinse well under cold running water and set aside.

Peel the lime and cut lengthwise in half. Set aside.

Wash the basil and roughly torn it with hands. Set aside.

Now, combine watermelon, blueberries, lime, and basil in a juicer. Process until juiced. Transfer to a serving glass and stir in the cayenne pepper and water.

Refrigerate for 10 minutes before serving.

Nutritional information per serving: Kcal: 198, Protein: 4.1g, Carbs: 58.7g, Fats: 1.4g

10. Carrot Plum Juice

Ingredients:

1 cup of baby carrots, sliced

4 whole plum, chopped

1 cup of Romaine lettuce, shredded

1 cup of mustard greens, torn

1 oz of water

Preparation:

Wash and peel the carrots. Cut into thin slices and fill the measuring cup. Reserve the rest in the refrigerator.

Wash the plums and cut each in half. Remove the pits and set aside.

Combine lettuce and mustard greens in a large colander. Rinse well under cold running water. Shred the lettuce torn the mustard greens using hands. Set aside.

Now, combine carrots, plums, lettuce, and mustard greens in a juicer and process until juiced. Transfer to a serving glass and stir in the water.

Serve cold.

Nutritional information per serving: Kcal: 128, Protein: 4.8g, Carbs: 39.1g, Fats: 1.3g

11. Pepper Avocado Juice

Ingredients:

2 medium-sized red bell peppers, chopped

1 cup of avocado, sliced

1 cup of purple cabbage, chopped

1 whole leek, chopped

1 whole lime, peeled

Preparation:

Wash the peppers and cut in half. Remove the seeds and cut into small pieces. Set aside.

Peel the avocado and cut lengthwise in half. Cut into thin slices and reserve the rest in the refrigerator. Set aside.

Wash the cabbage thoroughly and chop into small pieces. Set aside.

Wash the leek and cut into bite-sized pieces. Set aside.

Peel the lime and cut lengthwise in half. Set aside.

Now, combine peppers, avocado, cabbage, leek, and lime in a juicer and process until juiced. Transfer to a serving glass and refrigerate for 15 minutes before serving.

Enjoy!

Nutritional information per serving: Kcal: 327, Protein: 8.1g, Carbs: 49.6g, Fats: 22.5g

12. Grapefruit Mango Juice

Ingredients:

1 whole grapefruit, peeled

1 cup of mango, cut into chunks

1 cup of fresh mint, roughly chopped

1 large banana, peeled

2 large strawberries, chopped

Preparation:

Peel the grapefruit and divide into wedges. Cut each wedge in half and set aside.

Peel the mango and cut into small chunks. Fill the measuring cup and reserve the rest in the refrigerator. Set aside.

Wash the mint roughly and torn with hands. Set aside.

Peel the banana and cut into small pieces. Set aside.

Wash the strawberries and remove the stems. Cut into bite-sized pieces and set aside.

Now, combine grapefruit, mango, mint, banana, and strawberries in a juicer and process until juiced. Transfer to a serving glass and add some ice cubes before serving.

Enjoy!

Nutritional information per serving: Kcal: 301, Protein: 5.9g, Carbs: 88.5g, Fats: 1.7g

13. Beet Lemon Juice

Ingredients:

1 whole beet, sliced

1 whole lemon, peeled

1 cup of cucumber, sliced

1 medium-sized orange, peeled

1 tbsp of liquid honey

Preparation:

Wash the beet and trim off the green parts. Cut into thin slices and set aside.

Peel the lemon and cut into quarters. Set aside.

Wash the cucumber and cut into thin slices. Fill the measuring cup and reserve the rest in the refrigerator.

Peel the orange and divide into wedges. Cut each wedge in half and set aside.

Now, combine beet, lemon, cucumber, and orange in a juicer and process until juiced. Transfer to a serving glass and stir in the honey.

Add some ice and serve immediately.

Nutritional information per serving: Kcal: 154, Protein: 3.5g, Carbs: 30.5g, Fats: 0.5g

14. Green Bean Juice

Ingredients:

1 cup of green beans, chopped

1 medium-sized Granny Smith's apple, cored

1 medium-sized celery stalk, cut into bite-sized pieces

1 cup of fresh spinach, chopped

Preparation:

Wash the green beans and chop into bite-sized pieces. Fill the measuring cup and reserve the rest for later.

Wash the apple and cut in half. Remove the core and cut into small chunks. Set aside.

Wash the celery and cut into bite-sized pieces. Set aside.

Wash the spinach thoroughly under cold running water. Chop into small pieces and fill the measuring cup. Reserve the rest for later.

Now, combine green beans, apple, celery, and spinach in a juicer and process until well juiced. Transfer to serving glass and add some ice before serving.

Enjoy!

Nutritional information per serving: Kcal: 140, Protein: 8.5g, Carbs: 37.3g, Fats: 1.4g

15. Pepper Kale Juice

Ingredients:

1 medium-sized red bell pepper, chopped

1 cup of fresh kale, chopped

1 cup of parsley, torn

1 large celery stalk, chopped

1 cup of cucumber, sliced

1 oz of water

Preparation:

Wash the bell pepper and cut lengthwise in half. Scrape out the seeds and remove the stem. Cut into bite-sized pieces and set aside.

Wash the kale thoroughly under cold running water. Slightly drain and chop it into small pieces. Set aside.

Wash the parsley and torn with hands. Fill the measuring cup and reserve the rest for later.

Wash the celery stalk and chop it into bite-sized pieces. Set aside.

Wash the cucumber and cut into thin slices. Fill the

measuring cup and reserve the rest for later.

Now, combine bell pepper, kale, parsley, celery, and cucumber in a juicer and process until juiced. Transfer to a serving glass and stir in the water. Add some ice and serve immediately.

Enjoy!

Nutritional information per serving: Kcal: 77, Protein: 6.6g, Carbs: 20.6g, Fats: 1.6g

16. Basil Zucchini Juice

Ingredients:

1 cup of fresh basil, chopped

1 medium-sized zucchini, sliced

1 whole lemon, peeled

1 whole lime, peeled

1 oz of water

Preparation:

Wash the basil thoroughly under cold running water. Slightly drain and chop into small pieces. Set aside.

Wash the zucchini and cut into thin slices. Set aside.

Peel the lemon and lime. Cut each fruit into quarters and set aside.

Now, combine basil, zucchini, lemon, and lime in a juicer. Process until well juiced. Transfer to a serving glass and stir in the water.

Refrigerate for 10 minutes before serving.

Nutritional information per serving: Kcal: 50, Protein: 3.9g, Carbs: 15.8g, Fats: 0.9g

17. Blueberry Grape Juice

Ingredients:

1 cup of blueberries

1 cup of black grapes

1 small Golden Delicious apple, cored

¼ tsp of cinnamon, ground

Preparation:

Wash the blueberries using a colander. Slightly drain and set aside.

Wash the grapes and fill the measuring cup. Reserve the rest for later.

Wash the apple and cut in half. Remove the core and cut into bite-sized pieces. Set aside.

Now, combine blueberries, grapes, and apple in a juicer and process until juiced. Transfer to a serving glass and stir in the cinnamon.

Add some ice before serving and enjoy!

Nutritional information per serving: Kcal: 191, Protein: 2.1g, Carbs: 54.7g, Fats: 1g

18. Mango Raspberry Juice

Ingredients:

1 cup of mango, chunked

1 cup of raspberries

1 small peach, pitted

3 whole apricots, chopped

Preparation:

Peel the mango and cut into small chunks. Fill the measuring cup and reserve the rest for later.

Wash the raspberries using a colander. Slightly drain and fill the measuring cup. Reserve the rest in the refrigerator or freezer for later.

Wash the peach and cut in half. Remove the pit and cut into bite-sized pieces. Set aside.

Wash the apricots and cut in half. Remove the pits and cut in quarters. Set aside.

Now, combine mango, raspberries, peach, and apricots in a juicer and process until juiced. Transfer to a serving glass refrigerate for 10 minutes before serving.

You can garnish with some fresh mint if you like, but it's optional.

Nutritional information per serving: Kcal: 206, Protein: 5.5g, Carbs: 63.5g, Fats: 2.1g

19. Pineapple Beet Juice

Ingredients:

1 cup of pineapple, chunked

1 whole beet, sliced

1 small orange, wedged

2 tbsp of coconut water

¼ tsp of ginger, ground

Preparation:

Cut the top of a pineapple and peel it using a sharp paring knife. Cut into small chunks and fill the measuring cup. Reserve the rest of the pineapple in a refrigerator.

Wash and trim off the beet. Cut into small slices and set aside.

Peel the orange and divide into wedges. Cut each wedge in half and set aside.

Now, combine pineapple, beet, and orange in a juicer and process until juiced. Transfer to a serving glass and stir in the coconut water and ginger.

Add some crushed ice and serve immediately.

Nutritional information per serving: Kcal: 135, Protein: 3.1g, Carbs: 40.7g, Fats: 0.5g

20. Kiwi Banana Juice

Ingredients:

3 whole kiwis, peeled

1 large banana, chopped

1 large strawberry, chopped

1 small apple, cored

¼ tsp of cinnamon, ground

Preparation:

Peel the kiwis and cut lengthwise in half. Set aside.

Peel the banana and chop into small chunks. Set aside.

Wash the strawberry and remove the stem. Cut into small pieces and set aside.

Wash the apple and cut in half. Remove the core and cut into bite-sized pieces. Set aside.

Now, combine kiwis, banana, strawberry, and apple in a juicer and process until juiced. Transfer to a serving glass and stir in the cinnamon.

Refrigerate for 10 minutes before serving.

Enjoy!

Nutritional information per serving: Kcal: 292, Protein: 4.4g, Carbs: 85g, Fats: 1.9g

21. Avocado Lemon Juice

Ingredients:

1 cup of avocado, cubed

1 whole lemon, peeled

1 cup of cranberries

1 cup of cucumber, sliced

1 cup of cherries, pitted

Preparation:

Peel the avocado and cut into small cubes. Fill the measuring cup and reserve the rest in the refrigerator. Set aside.

Peel the lemon and cut lengthwise in half. Set aside.

Wash the cranberries and set aside.

Wash the cucumber and cut into slices. Fill the measuring cup and reserve the the rest for later.

Wash the cherries and cut each in half. Remove the pits and set aside.

Now, combine avocado, cranberries, cucumber, and cherries in a juicer and process until juiced. Transfer to a serving glass and add some ice before serving.

Enjoy!

Nutritional information per serving: Kcal: 321, Protein: 5.8g, Carbs: 54.4g, Fats: 22.6g

22. Pomegranate Blackberry Juice

Ingredients:

1 cup of pomegranate seeds

1 cup of blackberries

1 whole lemon, peeled

1 medium-sized carrot, sliced

1 oz of water

Preparation:

Cut the top of the pomegranate fruit using a sharp paring knife. Slice down to each of the white membranes inside of the fruit. Pop the seeds into a measuring cup and set aside.

Wash the blackberries using a colander. Fill the measuring cup and reserve the rest. Set aside.

Peel the lemon and cut lengthwise in half. Set aside.

Wash and peel the carrot. Cut into thin slices and set aside.

Now, combine pomegranate seeds, blackberries, lemon, and carrot in a juicer. Process until juiced and transfer to a serving glass.

Add some ice or refrigerate for a while before serving.

Nutritional information per serving: Kcal: 119, Protein: 4.6g, Carbs: 41.3g, Fats: 2.1g

23. Celery Kale Juice

Ingredients:

1 cup of celery, chopped

1 cup of fresh kale, torn

1 cup of fresh mint, torn

1 whole lime, peeled

1 small Granny Smith's apple, cored

Preparation:

Wash the celery and chop into small pieces. Fill the measuring cup and set aside.

Combine kale and mint in a large colander. Wash thoroughly under cold running water. Slightly drain and torn with hands. Set aside.

Peel the lime and cut into small pieces. Set aside.

Wash the apple and cut in half. Remove the core and cut into bite-sized pieces. Set aside.

Now, combine celery, kale, mint, lime, and apple in a juicer and process until juiced. Transfer to a serving glass and add some ice before serving.

Enjoy!

Nutritional information per serving: Kcal: 121, Protein: 5.3g, Carbs: 35.8g, Fats: 1.3g

24. Potato Zucchini Juice

Ingredients:

1 cup of sweet potatoes, cubed

1 small zucchini, sliced

1 small apple, cored

¼ tsp of ginger, ground

Preparation:

Peel the sweet potato and cut into small cubes. Fill the measuring cup and reserve the rest for later.

Peel the zucchini and cut into thin slices. Set aside.

Wash the apple and cut in half. Remove the core and cut into bite-sized pieces. Set aside.

Now, combine sweet potatoes, zucchini, and apple in a juicer. Process until well juiced. Transfer to a serving glass and stir in the ginger.

Refrigerate for 10 minutes before serving.

Enjoy!

Nutritional information per serving: Kcal: 181, Protein: 4.2g, Carbs: 50.1g, Fats: 0.7g

25. Apricot Plum Juice

Ingredients:

2 whole apricots, pitted

2 whole plums, chopped

1 cup of cherries, pitted

1 small orange, peeled

1 tbsp of coconut water

Preparation:

Wash the apricots and cut in half. Remove the pits and cut all into small pieces. Set aside.

Wash the plums and cut in half. Remove the pits and cut into bite-sized pieces. Set aside.

Wash the cherries using a colander. Remove the pits and set aside.

Peel the orange and divide into wedges. Cut each wedge in half and set aside.

Now, combine apricots, plums, cherries, and orange in a juicer and process until well juiced. Transfer to a serving glass and stir in the coconut water.

Refrigerate for 10 minutes before serving.

Enjoy!

Nutritional information per serving: Kcal: 191, Protein: 4.3g, Carbs: 56.3g, Fats: 1.1g

26. Fennel Broccoli Juice

Ingredients:

1 cup of fennel, chopped

1 cup of broccoli, chopped

1 cup of Brussels sprouts, halved

1 cup of watercress, torn

1 cup of cucumber, sliced

Preparation:

Wash the fennel and trim off the outer leaves. Using a sharp paring knife, cut into small pieces and fill the measuring cup. Reserve the rest for later.

Wash the broccoli and cut into small pieces. Fill the measuring cup and reserve the rest in the refrigerator. Set aside.

Wash the Brussels sprouts and trim off the outer layers. Cut in half and set aside.

Wash the watercress thoroughly under cold running water. Slightly drain and torn with hands. Set aside.

Wash the cucumber and cut into thin slices. Fill the

measuring cup and reserve the rest for later.

Now, combine fennel, broccoli, Brussels sprouts, watercress, and cucumber in a juicer and process until juiced. Transfer to a serving glass and refrigerate for 10 minutes before serving.

Enjoy!

Nutritional information per serving: Kcal: 72, Protein: 7.7g, Carbs: 22.6g, Fats: 0.8g

27. Cranberry Pear Juice

Ingredients:

1 cup of cranberries

1 medium-sized pear, chopped

1 whole lemon, peeled

½ cup of strawberries, sliced

1 small ginger knob, peeled

1 oz of water

Preparation:

Wash the cranberries and fill the measuring cup. Set aside.

Wash the pear and cut in half. Remove the core and cut into small pieces. Set aside.

Peel the lemon and cut in half. Set aside.

Wash the strawberries and remove the stems. Cut into small pieces and fill the measuring cup. Set aside.

Peel the ginger knob and set aside.

Now, combine cranberries, pear, lemon, strawberries, and ginger in a juicer and process until juiced. Transfer to a serving glass and stir in the water.

Serve cold.

Nutritional information per serving: Kcal: 143, Protein: 2.4g, Carbs: 52.7g, Fats: 0.8g

28. Beet Green Carrot Juice

Ingredients:

1 cup of beet greens, torn

1 large carrot, sliced

1 medium-sized orange, peeled

1 cup of cantaloupe, chopped

¼ tsp of ginger, ground

Preparation:

Wash the beet greens thoroughly under cold running water. Drain and torn with hands. Set aside.

Wash the carrot and cut into thin slices. Set aside.

Peel the orange and divide into wedges. Cut each wedge in half and set aside.

Cut the cantaloupe in half. Scoop out the seeds and cut one large wedge. Peel it and cut into small pieces. Fill the measuring cup and reserve the rest of the cantaloupe in a refrigerator.

Now, combine beet greens, carrot, orange, and cantaloupe in a juicer and process until juiced. Transfer to a serving glass and stir in the ginger.

Serve cold.

Nutritional information per serving: Kcal: 99, Protein: 3.5g, Carbs: 30.5g, Fats: 0.6g

29. Collard Greens Cucumber Juice

Ingredients:

2 cups of collard greens, chopped

1 cup of cucumber, sliced

1 whole lime, peeled

1 cup of Swiss chard, chopped

1 large celery stalk, chopped

1 oz of water

¼ tsp of salt

Preparation:

Combine collard greens and Swiss chard in a large colander. Wash it under running water and slightly drain. Chop into small pieces and set aside.

Wash the cucumber and cut into thin slices. Fill the measuring cup and reserve the rest in the refrigerator.

Peel the lime and cut lengthwise in half. Set aside.

Wash the celery and cut into small pieces. Set aside.

Now, combine collard greens, cucumber, lime, Swiss chard,

and celery in a juicer and process until juiced. Transfer to a serving glass and stir in the water and salt. Refrigerate for 10 minutes before serving.

Enjoy!

Nutritional information per serving: Kcal: 40, Protein: 3.8g, Carbs: 12.7g, Fats: 0.7g

30. Pumpkin Pepper Juice

Ingredients:

1 cup of pumpkin, cubed

1 large yellow bell pepper, chopped

1 small zucchini, sliced

¼ tsp of cinnamon, ground

Preparation:

Cut the pumpkin lengthwise in half. Scoop out the seeds and cut one large wedge. Peel it and fill the measuring cup. Wrap the rest of the pumpkin in a plastic foil and refrigerate for later.

Wash the bell pepper and cut in half. Remove the seeds and stem. Cut into bite-sized pieces and set aside.

Wash the zucchini thoroughly and cut into thin slices. Set aside.

Now, combine pumpkin, bell pepper, and zucchini in a juicer and process until juiced. Transfer to a serving glass and stir in the cinnamon.

Refrigerate for 10 minutes before serving.

Enjoy!

Nutritional information per serving: Kcal: 86, Protein: 4.5g, Carbs: 22.9g, Fats: 0.9g

31. Kale Celery Juice

Ingredients:

1 cup of fresh kale, chopped

2 medium-sized celery stalk, chopped

1 small apple, cored

1 cup of Romaine lettuce, shredded

Preparation:

Wash the kale thoroughly under cold running water. Slightly drain and chop it into small pieces. Set aside.

Wash the celery stalks and cut into bite-sized pieces. Set aside.

Wash the apple and cut in half. remove the core and cut into small pieces. Set aside.

Wash the lettuce leaves and shred it. Fill the measuring cup and reserve the rest for later.

Now, combine kale, celery, apple, and lettuce in a juicer and process until juiced. Transfer to a serving glass and add some ice before serving.

Enjoy!

Nutritional information per serving: Kcal: 103, Protein: 4.6g, Carbs: 29.4g, Fats: 1.2g

32. Melon Lime Juice

Ingredients:

1 medium-sized wedge of honeydew melon

1 whole lime, peeled

1 small Granny Smith's apple, cored

1 large banana, peeled

¼ tsp of cinnamon, ground

Preparation:

Cut one large honeydew melon wedge and peel it. Remove the seeds and cut into bite-sized pieces. Wrap the rest of the melon in a plastic foil and refrigerate.

Peel the lime and cut lengthwise in half. Set aside.

Wash the apple and cut in half. Remove the core and cut into bite-sized pieces. Set aside.

Peel the banana and chop into small chunks. Set aside.

Now, combine melon, lime, apple, and banana in a juicer and process until juiced. Transfer to a serving glass and stir in the cinnamon.

Refrigerate for 10 minutes before serving.

Nutritional information per serving: Kcal: 226, Protein: 4.6g, Carbs: 29.4g, Fats: 1.2g

33. Guava Cherry Juice

Ingredients:

1 whole guava, peeled

1 cup of cherries, pitted

1 medium-sized orange, wedged

1 whole apricot, pitted

Preparation:

Peel the guava and cut into small chunks. Set aside.

Wash the cherries using a colander. Remove the stems and cut each in half. Remove the pits and fill the measuring cup. Set aside.

Peel the orange and divide into wedges. Cut each wedge in half and set aside.

Wash the apricot and cut in half. Remove the pit and cut into bite-sized pieces. Set aside.

Now, combine guava, cherries, orange, and apricot in a juicer and process until juiced. Transfer to a serving glass and add some ice.

Serve immediately.

Nutritional information per serving: Kcal: 173, Protein: 4.7g, Carbs: 51.8g, Fats: 1.1g

34. Mango Kiwi Juice

Ingredients:

1 cup of mango, chunked

1 whole kiwi, peeled

1 cup of fresh spinach, chopped

1 small ginger knob, peeled

2 tbsp of coconut water

Preparation:

Peel the mango and cut into small chunks. Fill the measuring cup and reserve the rest in the refrigerator.

Peel the kiwi and cut lengthwise in half. Set aside.

Wash the spinach thoroughly under cold running water. Slightly drain and chop it into small pieces. Set aside.

Peel the ginger knob and set aside.

Now, combine mango, kiwi, spinach, and ginger in a juicer and process until juiced. Transfer to a serving glass and stir in the coconut water. Refrigerate for 10 minutes before serving.

Enjoy!

Nutritional information per serving: Kcal: 190, Protein: 9.1g, Carbs: 53.6g, Fats: 2.2g

35. Pomegranate Plum Juice

Ingredients:

1 cup of pomegranate seeds

2 whole plums, pitted

1 small Golden Delicious apple, cored

1 large strawberry, chopped

Preparation:

Cut the top of the pomegranate fruit using a sharp paring knife. Slice down to each of the white membranes inside of the fruit. Pop the seeds into a measuring cup and set aside.

Wash the plums and cut lengthwise in half. Remove the pits and cut into small pieces. Set aside.

Wash the apple and cut in half. Remove the core and cut into bite-sized pieces. Set aside.

Wash the strawberry and remove the stem. Cut into small pieces and set aside.

Now, combine pomegranate seeds, plums, apple, and strawberry in a juicer and process until juiced. Transfer to a serving glass and add some crushed ice.

Serve immediately.

Nutritional information per serving: Kcal: 176, Protein: 2.8g, Carbs: 50.3g, Fats: 1.6g

36. Watermelon Cranberry Juice

Ingredients:

1 cup of watermelon, chopped

1 cup of whole cranberries

1 whole lemon, peeled

1 cup of fresh mint, chopped

1 tbsp of liquid honey

Preparation:

Cut the watermelon lengthwise. For one cup, you will need a large slice. Peel and cut into chunks. Remove the seeds and set aside. Reserve the rest for some other juices.

Wash the cranberries using a colander. Fill the measuring cup and reserve the rest in the refrigerator.

Peel the lemon and cut lengthwise in half. Set aside.

Wash the mint thoroughly under cold running water and roughly chop it. Set aside.

Now, combine watermelon, cranberries, lemon, and mint in a juicer and process until juiced. Transfer to a serving glass and stir in the honey.

Add few ice cubes and serve immediately.

Enjoy!

Nutritional information per serving: Kcal: 93, Protein: 2.9g, Carbs: 32.8g, Fats: 0.7g

37. Grape Pineapple Juice

Ingredients:

1 cup of black grapes

1 cup of pineapple, chunked

1 tsp of vanilla extract

Preparation:

In a heavy-bottomed pot, combine grapes and one cup of water. Bring it to a boil over a medium-high temperature, stirring occasionally. Stir in the vanilla extract and remove from the heat. Set aside to cool completely.

Cut the top of a pineapple fruit. Using a sharp paring knife, peel it and cut into thin slices. Fill the measuring cup and reserve the rest for later.

Now, combine grape mixture and pineapple in a juicer and process until well juiced. Transfer to a serving glass and refrigerate for 20 minutes before serving.

Garnish with some fresh mint, but it's optional.

Enjoy!

Nutritional information per serving: Kcal: 200, Protein: 2.1g, Carbs: 57g, Fats: 0.8g

38. Tomato Celery Juice

Ingredients:

5 cherry tomatoes, halved

1 large celery stalk, chopped

1 cup of cucumber, sliced

1 cup of fresh parsley, chopped

¼ tsp of salt

¼ tsp of black pepper, ground

½ tsp of Tabasco sauce

1 oz of water

Preparation:

Wash the cherry tomatoes and remove the stems. Cut each tomato in half and set aside.

Wash the celery stalk and chop it into bite-sized pieces. Set aside.

Wash the cucumber and cut into thin slices. Fill the measuring cup and reserve the rest for later.

Place the parsley in a colander and rinse it thoroughly.

Slightly drain and chop into small pieces. Set aside.

Now, combine cherry tomatoes, celery, cucumber, and parsley in a juicer and process until juiced. Transfer to a serving glass and stir in the salt, pepper, Tabasco sauce, and water.

Serve immediately!

Nutritional information per serving: Kcal: 38, Protein: 3.3g, Carbs: 10.9g, Fats: 0.8g

39. Blueberry Ginger Juice

Ingredients:

2 cups of blueberries

1 small ginger knob, peeled and chopped

1 medium-sized blood orange, peeled

1 cup of black grapes

Preparation:

Place the blueberries in a colander. Wash thoroughly under cold running water and drain. Fill the measuring cups and reserve the rest in the freezer.

Peel the ginger and cut into small pieces. Set aside.

Peel the orange and divide into wedges. Cut each wedge in half and set aside.

Wash the grapes and fill the measuring cup. Set aside.

Now, combine blueberries, ginger, orange, and grapes in a juicer and process until juiced. Transfer to a serving glass and add few ice cubes before serving.

Enjoy!

Nutritional information per serving: Kcal: 254, Protein: 4.1g, Carbs: 75.2g, Fats: 1.5g

40. Avocado Papaya Juice

Ingredients:

1 cup of avocado, cubed

1 small papaya, chopped

1 cup of cherries, halved

1 whole lemon, peeled

¼ tsp of cinnamon, ground

1 oz of water

Preparation:

Peel the avocado and cut lengthwise in half. Remove the pit and cut into small cubes. Fill the measuring cup and reserve the rest for later.

Peel the papaya and cut into small chunks. Set aside.

Peel the lemon and cut lengthwise in half. Set aside.

Now, combine avocado, papaya, and lemon in a juicer and process until juiced. Transfer to a serving glass and stir in the cinnamon and water.

Refrigerate for 15 minutes before serving and enjoy!

Nutritional information per serving: Kcal: 343, Protein: 5.8g, Carbs: 57.3g, Fats: 22.8g

41. Pumpkin Apple Juice

Ingredients:

1 cup of pumpkin, cubed

1 small Granny Smith's apple, cored

1 medium-sized carrot, sliced

1 cup of cucumber, sliced

¼ tsp of cinnamon, ground

¼ tsp of ginger, ground

Preparation:

Cut the pumpkin in half and scoop out the seeds. Wash it and cut one large wedge. Peel it and cut into small cubes. Fill the measuring cup and reserve the rest in the refrigerator.

Wash the apple and cut lengthwise in half. Remove the core and cut into small pieces. Set aside.

Wash and peel the carrot. Cut into thin slices and set aside.

Wash the cucumber and cut into thin slices. Fill the measuring cup and reserve the rest for later.

Now, combine pumpkin, apple, carrot, and cucumber in a

juicer and process until juiced. Transfer to a serving glass and stir in the cinnamon and ginger.

Refrigerate for 10 minutes before serving.

Nutritional information per serving: Kcal: 121, Protein: 2.7g, Carbs: 34.8g, Fats: 0.6g

42. Peach Lime Juice

Ingredients:

2 large peaches, pitted

1 whole lime, peeled

1 cup of apricots, sliced

1 large banana, peeled

Preparation:

Wash the peaches and cut in half. Remove the pits and cut each half into bite-sized pieces. Set aside.

Peel the lime and roughly chop it. Make sure to reserve lime juice while cutting.

Wash the apricots and cut in half. Remove the pits and cut into small pieces. Fill the measuring cup and set aside.

Peel the banana and cut into small chunks. Set aside.

Now, combine peaches, lime, apricots, and banana in a juicer and process until juiced. Transfer to a serving glass and add some crushed ice before serving.

Enjoy!

Nutritional information per serving: Kcal: 299, Protein: 7.2g, Carbs: 86.5g, Fats: 2g

43. Artichoke Spinach Juice

Ingredients:

1 medium-sized artichoke, chopped

1 cup of fresh spinach, chopped

1 cup of green beans, chopped

1 small green bell pepper, sliced

1 small ginger knob, peeled and sliced

Preparation:

Trim off the outer leaves of the artichoke using a sharp paring knife. Wash it and cut into bite-sized pieces. Set aside.

Using a colander, rinse the spinach thoroughly under cold running water. Chop into small pieces and set aside.

Place the beans in a deep pot. Add 1 cup of water and bring it to a boil. Cook for 5 minutes and remove from the heat. Set aside to cool completely.

Wash the bell pepper and cut in half. Remove the seeds and stem. Cut into small rings and set aside.

Peel the ginger knob and chop it into small pieces. Set

aside.

Now, combine artichoke, spinach, green beans, bell pepper, and ginger in a juicer and process until juiced. Transfer to a serving glass and refrigerate for 10 minutes before serving.

Nutritional information per serving: Kcal: 95, Protein: 11.9g, Carbs: 29.4g, Fats: 1.3g

44. Orange Pear Juice

Ingredients:

1 medium-sized orange, peeled

1 medium-sized pear, chopped

1 whole plum, pitted

1 whole lemon, peeled

1 oz of water

Preparation:

Peel the orange and divide into wedges. Cut each wedge in half and set aside.

Wash the pear and cut in half. Remove the core and chop into small pieces. Set aside.

Wash the plum and cut in half. Remove the pit and cut in small pieces.

Peel the lemon and cut into quarters. Set aside.

Now, combine orange, pear, plum, and lemon in a juicer and process until juiced. Transfer to a serving glass and stir in the water.

You can add a pinch of minced mint for some extra smooth

flavor, but it's optional.

Add some crushed ice and serve immediately.

Nutritional information per serving: Kcal: 166, Protein: 2.9g, Carbs: 55.4g, Fats: 0.8g

45. Carrot Grapefruit Juice

Ingredients:

2 medium-sized carrots, sliced

1 whole grapefruit, wedged

1 cup of Romaine lettuce, shredded

1 cup of fresh mint, chopped

1 whole lime, peeled

Preparation:

Wash and peel the carrots. Cut into thin slices and set aside.

Peel the grapefruit and divide into wedges. Cut each wedge in half and set aside.

Wash the lettuce thoroughly under cold running water. Shred it and fill the measuring cup. Reserve the rest for later.

Wash the mint and then place it in a medium bowl. Add one cup of hot water and let it soak for 10 minutes. Slightly drain and set aside.

Peel the lime and cut lengthwise in half. Set aside.

Now, combine carrots, grapefruit, lettuce, mint, and lime in a juicer and process until juiced. Transfer to a serving glass and add some crushed ice before serving.

Enjoy!

Nutritional information per serving: Kcal: 147, Protein: 4.7g, Carbs: 46.8g, Fats: 1.1g

46. Swiss Chard Juice

Ingredients:

2 cups of Swiss chard, chopped

1 cup of fresh kale, chopped

1 cup of collard greens, chopped

1 whole lemon, peeled

1 cup of cucumber, sliced

¼ tsp of ginger, ground

Preparation:

Combine Swiss chard, kale, and collard greens in a large colander. Wash thoroughly under cold running water. Slightly drain and roughly chop all. Set aside.

Peel the lemon and cut lengthwise in half. Set aside.

Wash the cucumber and cut into thin slices. Fill the measuring cup and reserve the rest in the refrigerator. Set aside.

Now, combine Swiss chard, kale, collard greens, lemon, and cucumber in a juicer. Process until juiced.

Transfer to a serving glass and stir in the ginger.

Serve cold.

Nutritional information per serving: Kcal: 57, Protein: 6.3g, Carbs: 17.8g, Fats: 1.2g

47. Broccoli Brussels Sprout Juice

Ingredients:

1 cup of broccoli, chopped

1 cup of Brussels sprouts, halved

1 cup of cucumber, sliced

1 whole lime, peeled

¼ tsp of ginger, ground

Preparation:

Wash the broccoli and trim off the outer layers. Cut into small pieces and fill the measuring cup. Set aside.

Wash the Brussels sprouts and trim off the outer leaves. Cut each sprout in half and fill the measuring cup. Reserve the rest for in the refrigerator.

Wash the cucumber and cut into thin slices. Fill the measuring cup and reserve the rest for later. Set aside.

Peel the lime and cut lengthwise in half.

Now, combine broccoli, Brussels sprouts, cucumber, and lime in a juicer and process until juiced. Transfer to a serving glass and stir in the ginger.

Add few ice cubes and serve immediately.

Nutritional information per serving: Kcal: 63, Protein: 6.1g, Carbs: 19.5g, Fats: 1.2g

48. Blackberry Avocado Juice

Ingredients:

2 cups of blackberries

1 cup of avocado, cubed

1 medium-sized apple, cored

¼ tsp of ginger, ground

Preparation:

Place the blackberries in a colander and wash thoroughly under cold running water. Slightly drain and set aside.

Peel the avocado and cut lengthwise in half. Remove the pit and cut into small cubes. Fill the measuring cup and reserve the rest in the refrigerator.

Wash the apple and cut in half. Remove the core and cut into bite-sized pieces. Set aside.

Now, combine blackberries, avocado, and apple in a juicer and process until juiced. Transfer to a serving glass and stir in the ginger.

Add some ice and serve immediately.

Nutritional information per serving: Kcal: 342, Protein: 7.7g, Carbs: 63.2g, Fats: 23.7g

49. Raspberry Pear Juice

Ingredients:

1 cup of raspberries

1 large pear, chopped

1 whole lemon, peeled

1 small green apple, cored

Preparation:

Wash the raspberries thoroughly using a colander. Slightly drain and set aside.

Wash the pear and cut in half. Remove the core and cut into bite-sized pieces. Set aside.

Peel the lemon and cut lengthwise in half. Set aside.

Wash the apple and cut in half. Remove the core and cut into small pieces. Set aside.

Now, combine raspberries, pear, lemon, and apple in a juicer and process until juiced. Transfer to a serving glass and add some ice before serving.

Enjoy!

Nutritional information per serving: Kcal: 214, Protein: 3.6g, Carbs: 74.7g, Fats: 1.6g

50. Coco Squash Juice

Ingredients:

1 cup of crookneck squash, sliced

1 medium-sized pear, chopped

1 cup of cucumber, sliced

1 whole lime, peeled

1 oz of coconut water

Preparation:

Peel the crookneck squash and scrape out the seeds with a spoon. Cut into small cubes and fill the measuring cup. Reserve the rest of the squash for some other recipe. Wrap in a plastic foil and refrigerate.

Wash the pear and cut in half. Remove the core and chop into small pieces. Set aside.

Wash the cucumber and cut into thin slices. Fill the measuring cup and reserve the rest in the refrigerator. Set aside.

Peel the lime and cut lengthwise in half. Set aside.

Now, combine squash, pear, cucumber, and lime in a juicer.

Process until juiced. Transfer to a serving glass and stir in the coconut water.

Add some ice and serve immediately.

Nutritional information per serving: Kcal: 120, Protein: 2.4g, Carbs: 37.6g, Fats: 0.7g

51. Kiwi Papaya Juice

Ingredients:

4 whole kiwis, peeled

2 small papaya, chopped

1 tbsp of fresh basil, roughly chopped

1 large banana, peeled

1 cup of cucumber, sliced

Preparation:

Peel the kiwis and cut in half. Set aside.

Peel the papaya and cut in half. Remove the seeds and dice into small pieces. Set aside.

Peel the banana and cut into chunks. Set aside.

Wash the cucumber and cut into thin slices. Fill the measuring cup and reserve the rest for later. Set aside.

Now, combine kiwis, papaya, basil, banana, and cucumber in a juicer and process until juiced. Transfer to a serving glass and add some ice before serving.

Enjoy!

Nutritional information per serving: Kcal: 365, Protein: 6.5g, Carbs: 107g, Fats: 2.8g

52. Pepper Broccoli Juice

Ingredients:

1 large red bell pepper, chopped

1 cup of broccoli, chopped

1 cup of cucumber, sliced

1 large celery stalk, chopped

¼ tsp of ginger, ground

Preparation:

Wash the pepper and cut in half. Remove the seeds and stem. Cut into thin slices and set aside.

Wash the broccoli and trim off the outer wilted layers. Cut into small pieces and set aside.

Wash the cucumber and cut into thin slices. Fill the measuring cup and reserve the rest in the refrigerator.

Wash the celery stalk and cut into small pieces. Set aside.

Now, combine pepper, broccoli, cucumber, and celery in a juicer and process until well juiced. Transfer to a serving glass and stir in the ginger.

Refrigerate for 10 minutes before serving.

Nutritional information per serving: Kcal: 71, Protein: 4.9g, Carbs: 19.7g, Fats: 1g

53. Cantaloupe Orange Juice

Ingredients:

1 cup of cantaloupe, diced

1 small orange, peeled

1 cup of fresh mint, torn

1 whole lemon, peeled

¼ tsp of ginger, ground

Preparation:

Cut the cantaloupe in half. Scoop out the seeds and cut one medium wedge. Peel it and dice into small pieces. Reserve the rest of the cantaloupe in a refrigerator.

Peel the orange and divide into wedges. Cut each wedge in half and set aside.

Wash the mint thoroughly under cold water. Slightly drain and torn with hands. Set aside.

Peel the lemon and cut lengthwise in half. Set aside.

Now, combine cantaloupe, orange, mint, and lemon in a juicer and process until juiced. Transfer to a serving glass and stir in the ginger.

Add some ice before serving and enjoy!

Nutritional information per serving: Kcal: 104, Protein: 3.8g, Carbs: 33.2g, Fats: 0.8g

54. Tomato Greens Juice

Ingredients:

7 cherry tomatoes, halved

2 cups of Swiss chard, torn

2 cups of collard greens, torn

1 cup of cucumber, sliced

1 whole leek, chopped

Preparation:

Wash the tomatoes and remove the stems. Cut each tomato in half and set aside.

Combine Swiss chard and collard greens in a large colander. Wash thoroughly under cold running water. Slightly drain and torn with hands. Set aside.

Wash the cucumber and cut into thin slices. Fill the measuring cup and reserve the rest for later.

Wash the leek and cut into small pieces. Set aside.

Now, combine tomatoes, Swiss chard, collard greens, cucumber, and leek in a juicer and process until juiced. Transfer to a serving glass and refrigerate for 10 minutes before serving.

Nutritional information per serving: Kcal: 91, Protein: 6.2g, Carbs: 25.7g, Fats: 1.1g

55. Mango Citrus Juice

Ingredients:

1 cup of mango, chunked

1 whole lemon, peeled

1 whole lime, peeled

1 small green apple, cored

1 tbsp of coconut water

¼ tsp of cinnamon, ground

Preparation:

Peel the mango and cut into small chunks. Fill the measuring cup and reserve the rest for later.

Peel the lemon and lime. Cut each fruit in half and set aside.

Wash the apple and cut in half. Remove the core and cut into bite-sized pieces. Set aside.

Now, combine mango, lemon, lime, and apple in a juicer and process until juiced. Transfer to a serving glass and stir in the coconut water and cinnamon.

Add some crushed ice and serve immediately.

Nutritional information per serving: Kcal: 178, Protein: 2.8g, Carbs: 53.4g, Fats: 1.1g

56. Beet Kale Juice

Ingredients:

1 whole beet, sliced

1 cup of fresh kale, torn

1 small green apple, cored

1 small orange, peeled

¼ tsp of ginger, ground

Preparation:

Wash and trim off the beet. Slightly peel and cut into thin slices. Set aside.

Place the kale in a colander and wash under running water. Drain and torn with hands. Set aside.

Wash the apple and cut in half. Remove the core and cut into bite-sized pieces. Set aside.

Peel the orange and divide into wedges. Cut each wedge in half and set aside.

Now, combine beet, kale, apple, and orange in a juicer and process until juiced. Transfer to a serving glass and stir in the ginger.

Add some crushed ice and serve immediately.

Nutritional information per serving: Kcal: 153, Protein: 5.7g, Carbs: 44.6g, Fats: 1.1g

57. Blueberry Kiwi Juice

Ingredients:

1 cup of blueberries

2 whole kiwis, peeled

1 whole lemon, peeled

1 cup of cantaloupe, diced

1 tbsp of coconut water

Preparation:

Place the blueberries in a colander. Wash thoroughly and drain. Set aside.

Peel the kiwis and lemon. Cut lengthwise in half and set aside.

Cut the cantaloupe in half. Scoop out the seeds and cut one large wedge. Peel it and cut into small pieces. Fill the measuring cup and reserve the rest of the cantaloupe in a refrigerator.

Now, combine blueberries, kiwis, lemon, and cantaloupe in a juicer and process until juiced. Transfer to a serving glass and stir in the coconut water.

Refrigerate for 10 minutes before serving.

Nutritional information per serving: Kcal: 196, Protein: 4.6g, Carbs: 59.8g, Fats: 1.6g

SALAD RECIPES

1. Buddha Bowl Salad

Ingredients:

½ cup drained chickpeas

¼ sliced avocado

½ sliced cucumber

1 cup baby spinach

1 sliced carrot

½ cup sliced radish

1 tbsp olive oil

Salt and pepper to taste

Preparation:

Rinse the chickpeas under running water using a colander. Drain and set aside.

Peel the avocado and cut lengthwise in half. Remove the pit and peel. Cut one half into two equal halves and thinly slice it. Set aside.

Rinse the baby spinach under running water and drain. Cut into small pieces and set aside.

Wash and peel the carrot. Cut into thin slices and set aside.

Now, combine all ingredients in a salad bowl and drizzle with olive oil, salt, and pepper.

Serve immediately.

Nutritional information per serving: Kcal: 451, Protein: 10.2g, Carbs: 38.9g, Fats: 26.4g

2. Egg Pepper Salad

Ingredients:

1 cup red bell pepper, chopped

4 large eggs

1 small tomato, chopped

1 tbsp olive oil

1 tsp balsamic vinegar

1 tbsp corn

Salt and pepper

Preparation:

Place the eggs in a heavy-bottomed pot and add water enough to cover. Bring to a boil and cook for 10 minutes. Using a slotted spoon, remove the eggs from the water and transfer to a bowl filled with ice cold water. Peel and chop into bite-sized pieces. Transfer to a large salad bowl and set aside.

Wash the tomato and chop into bite-sized pieces. Add to the bowl along with corn. Sprinkle all with olive oil, balsamic vinegar, salt, and pepper.

Stir until well combined and serve immediately.

Enjoy!

Nutritional information per serving: Kcal: 297, Protein: 16.1g, Carbs: 21.6g, Fats: 18.1g

3. Tuna Spinach Salad with Tomatoes and Onion

Ingredients:

2 cups canned tuna, drained

2 cups baby spinach, chopped

1 tomato, chopped

1 large onion, thinly sliced

1 tbsp olive oil

½ tsp dried thyme, ground

Salt and pepper to taste

Preparation:

Using a large colander, rinse the spinach under running water. Drain and chop into small pieces. Place in a large salad bowl and set aside.

Wash the tomato and chop into bite-sized pieces. Set aside.

Peel the onion and cut into thin slices. Set aside.

Now, combine spinach, tomatoes, and onion. Top with tuna and sprinkle all with thyme, salt, and pepper. Mix until well combined.

Refrigerate for 10-15 minutes before serving.

Nutritional information per serving: Kcal: 310, Protein: 47.4g, Carbs: 9.5g, Fats: 8.7g

4. Feta Beans Salad

Ingredients:

½ cup Feta cheese, crumbled

½ cup canned red beans, drained

1 cup Iceberg lettuce, torn

1 small red onion, chopped

1 small carrot, slices

1 tbsp olive oil

1 tbsp lime juice, freshly squeezed

Preparation:

Rinse the lettuce under running water. Drain and torn with your hands into small pieces. Place in a large salad bowl and set aside.

Peel the onion and slices into thin slices.

Rinse the carrot and trim off the ends. Cut into thin slices and set aside.

In a small mixing bowl, combine olive oil, lime juice, salt, and pepper. Optionally, add some cayenne pepper for some spicy aroma. Mix until well combined and set aside.

Now, combine all ingredients in a salad bowl and drizzle with previously prepared dressing. Mix and serve immediately

Enjoy!

Nutritional information per serving: Kcal: 342, Protein: 16.4g, Carbs: 36.3g, Fats: 15.6g

5. Creamy Spinach Salad

Ingredients:

2 cups spinach, choppe

¼ cup low-fat yogurt

1 garlic clove, minced

1 tbsp olive oil

¼ tsp cayenne pepper, ground

¼ tsp sea salt

Preparation:

Using a large colander, rinse the spinach thoroughly under running water. Drain and chop into small pieces.

Transfer the spinach into a steam basket. Pour 2 cups of water in a deep pot. Bring to a boil and place the steam basket on top of the pot. Steam for 10 minutes, or until the spinach has been completely wilted. Set aside.

In a small bowl, combine yogurt, garlic, olive oil, cayenne pepper, and salt. Mix until combined and set aside.

Now, transfer spinach to a serving dish and drizzle with previously prepared dressing. Mix and serve immediately.

Enjoy!

Nutritional information per serving: Kcal: 183, Protein: 5.5g, Carbs: 7.7g, Fats: 15.1g

6. Spicy Chickpea Salad

Ingredients:

1 cup canned chickpeas, drained and rinsed

1 small chili pepper, chopped

1 small red onion, chopped

1 medium-sized tomato, chopped

1 tbsp olive oil

1 tsp yellow mustard

Salt and pepper to taste

Preparation:

Using a small colander, rinse well the chickpeas. Drain and transfer to a large salad bowl. Set aside.

Cut the chili pepper lengthwise in half and remove the seeds. Chop into small pieces and set aside.

Peel the onion and chop into small pieces. Set aside.

Rinse the tomato and chop into bite-sized pieces. Set aside.

In a small bowl, combine oil, mustard, salt, and pepper. Mix until combined.

In a large bowl with chickpeas, add all the remaining ingredients. Drizzle all with oil mixture and give it a good stir.

Serve immediately.

Nutritional information per serving: Kcal: 301, Protein: 13.6g, Carbs: 44.4g, Fats: 8.9g

7. Warm Mushroom Rice Salad

Ingredients:

2 cups button mushrooms, sliced

½ cup brown rice

1 large tomato, chopped

1 tbsp fresh parsley, finely chopped

1 tbsp lime juice, freshly squeezed

1 tbsp olive oil

Salt and pepper

Preparation:

Place the rice in a heavy-bottomed pot. Add 1 cup of water and bring it to a boil. Reduce the heat to low and cook for 10-15 minutes, or until almost all the liquid has been evaporated. Remove from the heat and set let it chill for a while.

Meanwhile, wash the mushrooms and chop into small pieces. Set aside.

Preheat the oil in a nonstick skillet over a medium-high heat. Add mushrooms and cook for 4-5 minutes, or until all the liquid has been evaporated. Remove from the heat and set aside.

Now, combine previously cooked rice and mushrooms. Add chopped tomato, and parsley. Mix until well combined and sprinkle all with salt, pepper, and lime juice.

Stir once and serve immediately.

Nutritional information per serving: Kcal: 264, Protein: 6.6g, Carbs: 42.1g, Fats: 8.7g

8. Egg Almond Creme Salad

Ingredients:

5 large eggs

½ cup almonds, grated

1 cup cherry tomatoes, chopped

1 cup Greek yogurt

1 tbsp lemon juice

1 tbsp flaxseeds

Salt and pepper

Preparation:

Place the eggs in a deep pot and cover with water. Bring to a boil and then cook for 10-12 minutes. Remove immediately from the pot and transfer to a bowl with ice cold water. Let it chill for 2 minutes and peel.

Transfer the eggs to a food processor and add Greek yogurt, lemon juice, flaxseeds, salt, and pepper. Pulse until smooth and creamy.

Transfer the egg mixture to a serving bowl and top with grated almonds.

Refrigerate for at least 20 minutes before serving.

Enjoy!

Nutritional information per serving: Kcal: 285, Protein: 21.6g, Carbs: 9.8g, Fats: 18.4g

9. Carrot Lentil Salad

Ingredients:

4 large carrots, sliced

1 cup Greek yogurt

½ cup canned lentils

1 cup Iceberg lettuce, chopped

1 tbsp olive oil

1 tsp apple cider vinegar

Salt

Preparation:

Place the lentils in a colander and rinse under running water. Drain well and set aside.

Slightly peel the carrots and trim off the green ends. Cut into thin slices and set aside.

In a small bowl, combine Greek yogurt, olive oil, apple cider vinegar, and salt. Mix until combined and set aside.

In a large bowl, combine carrots, lentils, and lettuce. Drizzle all with yogurt mixture and give it a good stir. Refrigerate for 30 minutes before serving.

Enjoy!

Nutritional information per serving: Kcal: 368, Protein: 23.8g, Carbs: 47.9g, Fats: 9.6g

10. Couscous Salad

Ingredients:

¼ cup couscous

¼ eggplant, chopped

1 cup button mushrooms, sliced

¼ avocado, sliced

½ red bell pepper, chopped

1 cup broccoli

1 tbsp sesame oil

2 tbsp soy sauce

1 tsp mirin

¼ tsp salt

Preparation:

Place couscous in a pot and pour in enough water to barely cover. Stir well, sprinkle with salt, and bring to a boil. Reduce the heat to medium-low and cook for about 10 minutes. When done, remove from the heat and fluff with a fork. Cool for a while.

Meanwhile, grease a large wok pan with sesame oil and heat up. Add eggplant and broccoli. Sprinkle with salt and cook for 5-6 minutes

Now, add mushrooms, avocado, and red pepper. Sprinkle with mirin, soy sauce, and some more salt. Give it a good stir and continue to cook for 3-4 minutes

Finally, stir in couscous and cook for 2-3 more minutes.

Serve immediately.

Nutritional information per serving: Kcal: 504, Protein: 15.1g, Carbs: 61.9g, Fats: 24g

11. Grilled Peach Salad with Goat's Cheese

Ingredients:

1 sliced peach

1 cup baby spinach

1 cup arugula

3/4 cup goat's cheese

1 tsp coconut oil,

1 tbsp agave nectar

2 tbsp chopped walnuts

Preparation:

Preheat the grill to high heat.

Rinse the spinach thoroughly under running water. Drain and chop into small pieces. Set aside.

Slice peach into half-inch thick slices and brush with coconut oil.

Grill for 2-3 minutes on each side and transfer to a plate. Add the remaining ingredients and drizzle with agave nectar.

Toss to combine and serve immediately.

Nutritional information per serving: Kcal: 315, Protein: 12.5g, Carbs: 19g, Fats: 23g

12. French Beans Salad

Ingredients:

7 oz cooked french beans

1 cup sweet potato chunks

½ purple onion

½ sliced tomato

½ sliced carrot

1 chopped green chili

1 cup vegetable stock

1 tbsp oil

½ tsp curry powder

1 tsp cumin seeds

Salt and pepper to taste

Preparation:

Peel the potatoes and cut into small chunks. Reserve the rest in the refrigerator.

Peel the onion and cut into thin slices. Set aside.

Wash the tomato and chop into bite-sized pieces. Set aside.

Cut the chili lengthwise in half. Remove the seeds and chop into small pieces. Set aside.

Heat the oil in a large pan over medium-high heat. Add onions and carrots and cook for 4-5 minutes, stirring constantly.

Now, add green chili, tomato, cumin seeds, curry powder, salt, and pepper.Give it a good stir and continue to cook for 4-5 minutes. Finally, add the remaining ingredients and cook for 2 more minutes

Remove from the heat and let it cool completely before serving.

Nutritional information per serving: Kcal: 580, Protein: 9g, Carbs: 68.2g, Fats: 29.5g

13. Portobello Rice Salad

Ingredients:

½ cup rice

3 sliced Portobello mushrooms

1 tbsp sesame oil

2 tbsp soy sauce

½ tbsp sesame seeds

1 tsp honey

1 tbsp chopped parsley leaves

Salt and pepper to taste

Preparation:

Place rice in a heavy-bottomed pot and pour in 1 1/2 cup of water. Season with some salt and bring it to a boil. Reduce the heat to medium-low and simmer until all the liquid has evaporated. Stir occasionally.

When done, remove the rice from the heat and set aside.

Meanwhile, grease a non-stick skillet with some oil and heat up over medium-high heat. Add sliced mushrooms and season with salt and pepepr. Cook for 7-8 minutes, stirring occasionally.

Now add soy sauce, sesame seeds, honey, and parsley. Stir in the rice and continue to cook for 2 more minutes.

Remove from the heat and serve.

Nutritional information per serving: Kcal: 583, Protein: 18g, Carbs: 92g, Fats: 16g

14. Quinoa Salad with Grilled Cauliflower

Ingredients:

¼ cup quinoa

1 cup cauliflower florets

1 cup broccoli

½ sliced green pepper

1 cup cherry tomatoes

1 cup arugula

½ chopped purple onion

1 tbsp oil

½ tsp apple cider vinegar

Salt and to taste

Preparation:

Place quinoa in a fine mesh sieve and rinse well under cold running water. Transfer to a small saucepan and pour in 1/2 cup of water. Bring it to a boil and reduce the heat to low. Cook for 10 minutes, stirring constantly. Remove from the heat and cool. Set aside.

Now, brush a small grill pan with some oil and heat up over high heat. Add cauliflower and broccoli, sprinkle with some salt, and cook until tender and lightly charred. Remove from the heat and transfer to a bowl.

Stir in cooked quinoa and add vegetables. Sprinkle with oil, apple cider, and some salt to taste.

Serve immediately.

Nutritional information per serving: Kcal: 404, Protein: 14.3g, Carbs: 53.8g, Fats: 17.3g

15. Sweet Broccoli Salad

Ingredients:

1 cup broccoli florets

½ chopped tomato

1 cup chopped kale

½ cup shredded cabbage

2 tbsp chopped almonds

1 sliced orange,

2 tbsp agave nectar

¼ tsp ginger powder

Preparation:

Rinse the broccoli florets using a large colander. Drain and transfer to a large pot. Add water enough to cover and bring to a boil over medium-high heat. Cook for 5 minutes. Remove from the heat and drain well. Set aside.

Combine kale and cabbage in a large colander. Rinse well and drain. Chop into small pieces and set aside.

In a large bowl, combine tomatoes, kale, cabbage, orange, and broccoli. Top with almonds, agave nectar, and ginger.

Serve immediately.

Nutritional information per serving: Kcal: 294, Protein: 9.2g, Carbs: 55.9g, Fats: 6.4g

16. Asparagus Rice Salad with Lime

Ingredients:

¼ cup rice

3.5oz chopped asparagus

½ sliced cucumber

¼ cup drained green peas

1 tbsp sesame oil

2 tbsp freshly squeezed lime juice

Salt and pepper to taste

Preparation:

Place rice in a heavy-bottomed pot and pour in 3/4 cup of water. Sprinkle with some salt and bring it to a boil. Reduce the heat to medium and cook for 7-10 minutes, or until all the liquid has evaporated. Remove from the heat and cool to a room temperature. Set aside.

Grease a large skillet with oil and heat up over medium-high heat. Add asparagus and cook for 3-4 minutes, stirring constantly.

Now, add peas and season with some salt and pepper to

taste. Continue to cook for 2 minutes. Remove from the heat and transfer to a bowl. Stir in the chilled rice and add sliced cucumber.

Sprinkle with lime juice and serve immediately.

Nutritional information per serving: Kcal: 368, Protein: 8g, Carbs: 52.3g, Fats: 14.1g

17. Rice Mushroom Salad with Herbs

Ingredients:

½ cup rice

1 cup button mushrooms

2 crushed garlic cloves

1 chopped onion

½ tsp dried basil

¼ tsp dried marjoram

1 tsp dried celery

1 tbsp olive oil

Salt and pepper to taste

Preparation:

Place rice at the bottom of a small pot and pour in 1 1/2 cups of water. Sprinkle with salt and bring it to a boil. Reduce the heat to medium-low and simmer until all the liquid has evaporated. Remove from the heat and set aside.

Preheat the oven to 375 degrees F. Grease a small baking pan with oil and rice. Set aside.

Heat up the olive oil in a small skillet. Add onions and garlic. Sprinkle with some salt and cook until translucent. Add mushrooms and continue to cook for 3-4 minutes, stirring constantly. Sprinkle with herbs, salt, and pepper.

Transfer to a baking dish and pour in about 1/4 cup of water or vegetable stock. Bake for 15 minutes.

When done, remove from the oven and let chill completely before serving.

Nutritional information per serving: Kcal: 526, Protein: 10g, Carbs: 88.6g, Fats: 15.3g

18. Eggplant Kale Salad and Pine Nuts

Ingredients:

1 small eggplant

1 cup chopped kale

1 tbsp pine nuts

¼ cup feta cheese

2 tbsp Parmesan cheese

2 tbsp Greek yogurt

1 tbsp olive oil

¼ tsp garlic powder

Salt to taste

Preparation:

Slice eggplant lengthwise and generously sprinkle with salt. Place in a large sieve and let it sit for 15 minutes.

Meanwhile, preheat the oven to 400 degrees F. Line a small baking dish with some parchment paper and set aside.

In a medium-sized bowl, combine together kale, pine nuts, feta cheese, parmesan, Greek yogurt, garlic powder, and salt. Mix all well and set aside. Rinse eggplant under cold running water and scoop out most of the flesh.

Brush each half with oil and fill with the kale mixture. Bake for 25 minutes.

When done, remove from the oven set aside to cool completely before serving.

Enjoy!

Nutritional information per serving: Kcal: 466, Protein: 18g, Carbs: 38g, Fats: 31g

19. Zucchini Garlic Salad

Ingredients:

1 large zucchini

2 garlic cloves

1 tbsp olive oil

1 tbsp balsamic vinegar

1/4 tsp salt

Preparation:

Rinse zucchini under cold running water and slice into about 1/2-inch round slices. Sprinkle with salt and let it sit for 10 minutes.

Meanwhile, preheat the grill to high. Rinse the zucchini and pat dry with some kitchen paper.

In a small bowl, whisk together olive oil, balsamic vinegar, salt, and garlic powder.

Brush zucchini with this mixture and grill for 3-4 minutes per side.

When done, let it chill completely before serving.

Enjoy!

Nutritional information per serving: Kcal: 163, Protein: 3.3g, Carbs: 8.4g, Fats: 13.8g

20. Mushroom Leek Salad with Rice

Ingredients:

½ cup brown rice

1 chopped leek

1 cup sliced mushrooms

1 chopped onion

1 chopped spring onion

1 chopped celery stalk

1 tbsp olive oil

2 tbsp soy sauce

1 tsp balsamic vinegar

¼ tsp dried basil

½ tsp salt

½ tsp red pepper flakes

Preparation:

Boil rice according to package instructions. Remove from the heat and set aside.

Heat up the oil in a wok pan and add chopped onions, spring onion, leek, and celery stalk. Sprinkle with some salt and cook for 4-5 minutes, stirring constantly.

Now, add mushrooms, soy sauce, and balsamic vinegar. Sprinkle with red pepper flakes, salt, basil, and optionally some pepper to taste. Continue to cook for 5 minutes, stirring occasionally.

Finally, add rice and give it a good stir.

Optionally, sprinkle all with finely chopped parsley and serve immediately.

Enjoy!

Nutritional information per serving: Kcal: 603, Protein: 14.2g, Carbs: 101g, Fats: 16.7g

21. Boiled Potato Salad with Mustard Seeds and Parsley

Ingredients:

1 large potato

1 sliced onion

1 crushed garlic clove

1 tbsp mustard seeds

1 tbsp finely chopped parsley

1 tbsp olive oil

2 tbsp lemon juice

Salt and pepper to taste

Preparation:

Peel potato and rinse well under cold running water. Cut into bite-sized pieces and place in a small pot. Pour in enough water to cover and bring it to a boil. Reduce the heat to medium and cook until fork tender. Remove from the heat and drain. Transfer to a bowl and cool for a while.

Meanwhile, peel and slice onion. Sprinkle with some salt and let it sit for 5 minutes. Rinse well and drain.

Transfer to a bowl along with garlic, mustard seeds, and parsley. Sprinkle with some salt and pepper to taste and drizzle with olive oil and lemon juice.

Serve cold.

Nutritional information per serving: Kcal: 361, Protein: 8.2g, Carbs: 45.8g, Fats: 18.6g

22. Russian Vegetable Salad

Ingredients:

1 cup cooked beets

1 chopped tomato

1 chopped spring onion

1 tbsp salted capers

1 tbsp olive oil

1 tbsp lemon juice

Salt and pepper to taste

Preparation:

Trim and peel the beets. Cut into thin slices and place in a deep pot. Sprinkle with some salt and water enough to cover. Bring to a boil and cook for 10 minutes, or until soften. Remove from the heat and drain the water. Let it chill completely.

Wash the tomato and chop into bite-sized pieces. Place in a large bowl and set aside.

Chop the spring onions into small pieces and add it to the bowl with tomatoes.

In a small mixing bowl, combine capers, olive oil, lemon juice, salt, and pepper. Mix until well combined and set aside.

Finally, add beets to the bowl and drizzle all with the previously prepared dressing. Mix and serve immediately.

Enjoy!

Nutritional information per serving: Kcal: 264, Protein: 4.2g, Carbs: 21.4g, Fats: 15.1g

23. Chickpea Sun Dried Tomato Salad

Ingredients:

1/3 cup roasted chickpeas

1 cup sun-dried tomatoes

¼ cup cooked quinoa

1 sliced cucumber

½ sliced red bell pepper

1 tbsp olive oil

1 tsp lemon juice

Salt and pepper to taste

Preparation:

Preheat the oven to 350 degrees. Line some parchment paper over a baking sheet and set aside.

Drain but don't rinse chickpeas. Sprinkle with some salt and transfer to baking sheet. Roast for 20-25 minutes or until golden brown. Remove from the oven and cool for a while.

Meanwhile, prepare the remaining ingredients. Place quinoa in a small pot and pour in 1/2 cup of water. Generously sprinkle with some salt and bring it to a boil.

Simmer for 10 minutes over medium heat, stirring occasionally. Remove from the heat and cool for a while.

Slice cucumber lengthwise and place in a bowl. Add the remaining ingredients and drizzle with olive oil and lemon juice.

Season with some salt and pepper to taste and serve immediately.

Nutritional information per serving: Kcal: 368, Protein: 10.1g, Carbs: 49.7g, Fats: 17.3g

24. Halloumi Cheese Salad

Ingredients:

3oz Halloumi cheese

1 orange

1 cup arugula

¼ cup pomegranate seeds

1 tbsp oil

1 tbsp orange juice

Salt

Preparation:

Grease a non-stick grill pan with oil and heat up over medium high heat. Slice the cheese into approximately 1/4-inch thick slices and grill for about 3 minutes on each side.

Sprinkle with salt and remove from the pan.

In a medium bowl, combine the remaining ingredients and add cheese. Sprinkle with orange juice and optionally some more salt.

Serve immediately.

Nutritional information per serving: Kcal: 553, Protein: 20.5g, Carbs: 32.4g, Fats: 39.4g

25. Grilled Peach Salad with Blue Cheese and Walnuts

Ingredients:

1 sliced peach

1 sliced purple onion

2 oz blue cheese

1 cup arugula

1oz walnuts

2 tbsp soy sauce

2 tsp rice vinegar

1 tsp orange zest

2 tsp black sesame seeds

¼ tsp ginger powder

Preparation:

Rinse the arugula thoroughly under running water using a large colander. Drain and torn into small pieces. Set aside.

Peel the onion and cut into thin slices. Set aside.

In a small bowl, whisk together soy sauce, rice vinegar, orange zest, sesame seeds, and ginger powder. Set aside.

Preheat a non-stick grill pan or an electric grill over high heat. Slice peach into 1/4-inch thich slices and brush with the soy sauce mixture. Grill for 3-4 minutes on one side. Carefully flip each piece and continue to grill for 2 more minutes.

Remove from the heat and place in a bowl. Add onions, blue cheese, arugula, and walnuts. Toss to combine and serve immediately.

Nutritional information per serving: Kcal: 543, Protein: 24.5g, Carbs: 33g, Fats: 37.2g

26. Moroccan Rice Salad

Ingredients:

¼ cup long grain rice

¼ cup drained lentils

1 cup sliced button mushrooms

2 chopped onions

¼ tsp cumin powder

¼ tsp cayenne pepper

¼ tsp smoked paprika

2 tbsp raisins

Preparation:

Preheat the oven to 350 degrees F.

Place rice in a small saucepan and pour in 1/2 cup of water. Sprinkle with some salt and bring it to a boil. Reduce the heat to medium-low and simmer until all the liquid has evaporated. Stir well and remove from the heat. Set aside.

Now, grease a small skillet with some oil and add onions. Sprinkle with cumin powder, cayenne pepper, and smoked paprika. Cook until translucent. Stir in mushrooms and continue to cook for 5 minutes, stirring occasionally. Stir in lentils and remove from the heat.

In a large bowl, combine together rice and the lentil mixture. Optionally, sprinkle with some more spices and place in a small baking pan. Add raisins and cook for 15-20 minutes.

When done, set aside to cool completely before serving.

Nutritional information per serving: Kcal: 495, Protein: 21.3g, Carbs: 103g, Fats: 1.2g

27. Vegetable Saute Salad

Ingredients:

1 chopped potato

½ chopped sweet potato

1 chopped red bell pepper

1 cup sliced cherry tomatoes,

1 chopped onion

1 garlic clove

2 tbsp flour

1 tsp cayenne pepper

1/2 tsp dried basil

1/2 tsp salt

1/2 cup vegetable stock

1/4 cup finely chopped parsley

1 tbsp olive oil

Preparation:

Heat the oil in a large non-stick frying pan. Add onions and garlic. Stir all well and cook until translucent.

Now, add potatoes and pour in vegetable stock. Season with salt, cayenne, and basil. Cook over medium heat until fork tender and then add sweet potato, red bell pepper, and cherry tomato. Stir in parsley and continue to cook until completely soft.

If necessary, add some more water or vegetable stock and stir in flour. Cook for 2-3 minutes and remove from the heat.

Cool completely before serving and enjoy!

Nutritional information per serving: Kcal: 487, Protein: 11.4g, Carbs: 82.3g, Fats: 15.2g

28. Black Bean Salad

Ingredients:

¼ cup rice

¼ cup black beans, soaked overnight

¼ small chopped red bell pepper

1 tsp olive oil

1 minced garlic clove

1 tbsp finely chopped cilantro

¼ tsp dried rosemary

¼ tsp smoked paprika

¼ tsp ground black pepper

1/8 tsp salt

Preparation:

Place the rice in a heavy-bottomed pot and cover with 3/4 cup of water. Bring it to a boil and then reduce the heat to low. Cook for 13-15 minutes.

Meanwhile, rinse and drain the beans. Place in a deep pot and cover with 1 cup of water. Bring it to a boil and cook for 20 minutes.

When done, drain well and set aside.

Preheat the oil in a large skillet over a medium-high heat. Add garlic and stir-fry for 2 minutes. Add beans, rice, and bell pepper. Sprinkle with rosemary, paprika, salt, and pepper. Stir well and cook for 3-4 minutes, stirring occasionally.

When done, remove from the heat and let it cool completely.

Serve cold.

Nutritional information per serving: Kcal: 421, Protein: 15g, Carbs: 78g, Fats: 6.2g

29. Mushroom Pepper Salad

Ingredients:

1 cup sliced button mushrooms

1 medium-sized chopped red bell pepper

¼ cup chopped broccoli

1 tbsp sesame seeds

1 tsp avocado oil

½ tsp rice vinegar

1 tsp soy sauce

¼ tsp chili powder

¼ tsp dried thyme

1/8 tsp ginger powder

1/8 tsp salt

Preparation:

Wash the pepper and cut lengthwise in half. Remove the seeds and cut into bite-sized pieces. Set aside.

Preheat the avocado oil in a large skillet over a medium-high heat. Add mushrooms and cook for 5 minutes, stirring occasionally.

Add chopped pepper and broccoli. Sprinkle with salt, thyme, and chili powder. Stir well and cook for 3-4 minutes.

Stir in the sesame seeds, soy sauce, vinegar, and ginger powder. Cook for 1 more minute and remove from the heat.

When chilled completely, add some more vinegar and serve.

Nutritional information per serving: Kcal: 127, Protein: 6.2g, Carbs: 15.9g, Fats: 6.3g

30. Tabbouleh Salad

Ingredients:

¼ cup bulgur

3 halved cherry tomatoes

¼ cup finely chopped cilantro

¼ cup sliced cucumber

1 tsp olive oil

2 tbsp finely chopped fresh mint

1 tsp lemon juice

1/8 tsp salt

1/8 tsp ground black pepper

Preparation:

Place bulgur in a deep bowl and pour in 1/2 cup of boiling water. Add olive oil and give it a good stir. Cover with a lid and let it stand for 20 minutes.

Now, combine all the remaining ingredients in a large salad bowl. Add bulgur and stir until well incorporated.

Optionally, add a pinch of red pepper or cayenne for spicier aroma.

Nutritional information per serving: Kcal: 231, Protein: 8.2g, Carbs: 41.6g, Fats: 5.7g

31.   Zucchini Carrot Salad with Potatoes

Ingredients:

¼ cup sliced zucchini

1 medium-sized sliced carrot

1 large chopped potato

1 large sliced red bell pepper

¼ cup chopped eggplant

1 small chopped onion

1 finely chopped garlic clove

1 tsp olive oil

1 tsp soy sauce

1/8 tsp dried marjoram

1/8 tsp dried celery

1/8 tsp salt

1/8 tsp ground black pepper

Preparation:

First, wash and prepare the vegetables.

Peel the zucchini and carrot. Cut into thin slices and set aside.

Wash the bell pepper and cut lengthwise in half. Remove the seeds and stems. Cut into thin slices and set aside.

Combine eggplant, zucchini, potato, and carrot in a heavy bottomed pot. Add water enough to cover and sprinkle with some salt. Bring it to a boil and cook for 5 minutes. Remove from the heat and drain well.

In a small saucepan, heat up the olive oil over a medium-high heat. Add garlic and onions and stir-fry for 3-4 minutes. Add all the ingredients and cook for 5-7 minutes, stirring occasionally.

Remove from the heat and serve immediately.

Nutritional information per serving: Kcal: 433, Protein: 11g, Carbs: 90g, Fats: 6.3g

32. Apple Spinach Salad

Ingredients:

1 large Granny Smith's apple, cored and chopped

1 cup chopped spinach

1 cup chopped arugula

1 cup low fat cream

1 tsp apple cider vinegar

¼ tsp Italian seasoning

1 tbsp chopped walnuts

Salt and pepper

Preparation:

In a mixing bowl, combine low fat cream, apple cider vinegar, Italian seasoning, salt, and pepper. Mix until well combined and set aside.

Wash the apple and cut in half. Remove the core and cut into thin slices. Set aside.

In a large colander, combine spinach and arugula. Rinse under running water and drain. Set aside.

Now, combine apple, spinach, and arugula in a large salad bowl. Drizzle all with creamy dressing and give it a good stir.

Serve immediately.

Nutritional information per serving: Kcal: 461, Protein: 11.8g, Carbs: 57.8g, Fats: 21.6g

33. Mediterranean Fish Salad

Ingredients:

4 oz mackerel fillets

1 cup cherry tomatoes

¼ cup green olives, sliced

1 small sliced onion

1 tbsp lemon juice

½ tsp ground basil

¼ tsp ground garlic

¼ tsp ground rosemary

1 tbsp olive oil

Salt and pepper

Preparation:

Preheat the oven to 350 degrees. Line a piece of parchment paper over a baking sheet and set aside.

In a small mixing bowl, combine rosemary, olive oil, salt, and pepper. Mix until combined and set aside.

Rinse the fillets under running water and pat-dry with a

kitchen paper. Generously sprinkle with previously prepared mixture. Bake for 20 minutes, turning once halfway through. Remove from the oven and set aside to chill for a while.

Usinge a kitchen paper, soak up the excess oil and chop the fillets into bite-sized pieces.

Now, combine fish with the remaining ingredients on a serving plate and drizzle with the remaining olive oil mixture.

Give it a good stir and serve immediately.

Nutritional information per serving: Kcal: 486, Protein: 29.6g, Carbs: 14.5g, Fats: 35.1g

34. Tuna Kalamata Salad

Ingredients:

1 cup canned tuna

½ cup Kalamata olives, sliced

1 cup chopped Iceberg lettuce

1 small sliced red onion

1 chopped red bell pepper

1 tbsp olive oil

1 tbsp lemon juice

½ tsp Italian seasoning

Salt and red pepper

Preparation:

Using a large colander, rinse the lettuce under running water. Drain and torn with your hands into a small pieces. Place in a large salad bowl and set aside.

Remove the pits from olives and cut into thin slices.

Peel the onion and cut into thin slices.

Wash the bell pepper and cut lengthwise in half. Remove

the seeds and stem. Cut into small pieces and set aside.

In a small mixing bowl, combine olive oil, lemon juice, Italian seasoning, salt, and pepper. Mix until combined and set aside.

Now, combine lettuce, onion, and red bell pepper in a large salad bowl. Top with tuna and drizzle with previously prepared dressing.

Serve immediately.

Nutritional information per serving: Kcal: 306, Protein: 25.1g, Carbs: 11g, Fats: 18.4g

35. Green Bean Spinach Salad with Walnuts

Ingredients:

1 cup fresh baby spinach

1 cup green beans

1 garlic clove

2 tbsp chopped walnuts

1 tsp sunflower oil

Salt to taste

Preparation:

Rinse the green beans under running water. Drain and chop into bite-sized pieces. Transfer to a large pot and cover with water. Bring to a boil over medium-high heat. Cook for 10 minutes. Remove from the heat. Using a slotted spoon, drain and set aside to chill for a while.

Rinse the spinach using a colander. Drain well and torn into small pieces. Transfer to a large bowl and add green beans.

Drizzle with sunflower oil and minced garlic. Sprinkle with some salt and stir well.

Top with walnuts before serving.

Nutritional information per serving: Kcal: 183, Protein: 6.8g, Carbs: 11.5g, Fats: 14.1g

36. Quinoa Radish Salad

Ingredients:

½ cup quinoa

1 cup chopped radish

½ cup grated cabbage

½ cup feta cheese

1 tbsp finely chopped parsley

¼ tsp cayenne pepper

1 tsp balsamic vinegar

Olive oil

Salt to taste

Preparation:

In a heavy-bottomed pot, combine quinoa and 1 cup of water. Bring to a boil over medium-high heat. Reduce the heat to low and cook for 10-12 minutes, or until all the liquid has been evaporated. Remove from the heat and fluff with a fork. Set aside.

Trim off the outer leaves of radish. Rinse well under running water and transfer to a cutting board. Chop into thin strips and sprinkle with some vinegar.

In a large salad bowl, combine quinoa, radish, cabbage, and feta cheese. Sprinkle all with olive oil, salt, cayenne pepper, and parsley.

Give it a good stir and serve immediately.

Nutritional information per serving: Kcal: 271, Protein: 12g, Carbs: 32.1g, Fats: 10.7g

37. Sweet Potato Cheese Salad

Ingredients:

1 medium sweet potato

1 large onion

1 cup cottage cheese

1 tbsp olive oil

1 tbsp finely chopped parsley

Salt and pepper to taste

Preparation:

Peel the sweet potato and cut into small chunks. Place in a deep pot and add water enough to cover. Bring to a boil and cook for 10-15 minutes, or until fork-tender. Remove from the heat and drain well. Set aside to cool completely.

Peel the onion and cut into small pieces. Sprinkle with salt and let it stand for 10 minutes. Using a colander, rinse well and drain. Transfer to a large salad bowl along with sweet potato chunks and cottage cheese.

Sprinkle with olive oil, parsley, salt, and pepper. Mix until all well incorporated and serve immediately.

Enjoy!

Nutritional information per serving: Kcal: 488, Protein: 35.1g, Carbs: 46g, Fats: 18.7g

38. Creamy Broccoli Pepper Salad

Ingredients:

1 cup chopped broccoli

1 cup Greek yogurt

1 small green pepper

½ tsp garlic powder

1 tbsp olive oil

1 tsp ground basil

Salt to taste

Preparation:

Using a large colander, rinse the broccoli under running water. Drain and chop into bite-sized pieces. Set aside.

Preheat the oil in a frying pan over a medium-high heat. Add broccoli and sprinkle with some salt. Cook for 10 minutes, or until soften. Remove from the heat and set aside to cool.

In a food processor, combine green pepper, Greek yogurt, garlic, basil, and salt. Pulse until smooth and creamy.

Drizzle the broccoli with yogurt mixture and give it a good

stir.

Refrigerate for 20 mintues before serving.

Nutritional information per serving: Kcal: 323, Protein: 23.7g, Carbs: 19g, Fats: 18.5g

39. Lentil Cucumber Salad

Ingredients:

1 cup canned lentils

1 small cucumber

¼ cup low fat cream

2 tbsp lemon juice

2 tbsp olive oil

1 tbsp finely chopped parsley

1 large tomato

1 small onion

1 minced garlic clove

½ tsp dried dill

Salt to taste

Preparation:

Wash the cucumber and cut into small chunks. Place in a food processor along with low fat cream, lemon juice, olive oil, garlic, dill, and salt. Pulse until smooth and creamy and set aside.

Wash the tomato and cut into bite-sized pieces. Set aside.

Peel the onion and cut into thin rings. Set aside.

In a large bowl, combine lentils, tomato, and onion. Pour over the creamy mixture and give it a good stir.

Refrigerate for 30 minutes before serving.

Enjoy!

Nutritional information per serving: Kcal: 323, Protein: 23.7g, Carbs: 19g, Fats: 18.5g

40. Creamy Egg Salad

Ingredients:

4 large eggs

1 cup cottage cheese

1 tbsp sour cream

1 large tomato

1 large purple onion

1 tbsp lemon juice

1 tbsp minced hazelnuts

Salt to taste

Preparation:

Place the eggs in a deep pot and add water enough to cover. Bring to a boil over medium-high heat. Cook for 10-12 minutes and remove from the heat. Using a slotted spoon, transfer to separate bowl with ice cold water. Let it cool for 2 minutes and then peel. Chop into small pieces and set aside.

Wash the tomato and cut into bite-sized pieces. Set aside.

Peel the lemon and cut into thin rings. Set aside.

In a mixing bowl, combine cottage cheese, sour cream, lemon juice, and salt. Optionally, add some herbs according to your taste. Mix until well combined and set aside.

Ina large bowl, combine eggs, tomatoes, and onion. Pour over the cheese mixture and give it a good stir. Mix until well combined and refrigerate for 20 minutes before serving.

Enjoy!

Nutritional information per serving: Kcal: 320, Protein: 30.3g, Carbs: 16.2g, Fats: 15.1g

41. Arugula Tomato Salad

Ingredients:

2 cups chopped arugula

2 medium-sized tomatoes

¼ cup crumbled feta cheese

1 tbsp lemon juice

1 minced garlic clove

½ tsp dried thyme

Salt and pepper to taste

Preparation:

Using a large colander, rinse the arugula under running water. Drain well and chop into small pieces. Set aside.

Rinse the tomatoes well and transfer to a cutting board. Cut into bite-sized pieces and set aside.

In a small mixing bowl, combine lemon juice, garlic clove thyme, olive oil, salt, and pepper. Mix until well combined and set aside.

In a large salad bowl, combine arugula, tomatoes, and feta cheese. Drizzle with previously prepared dressing and give it a good stir.

Refrigerate for 15 minutes before serving.

Nutritional information per serving: Kcal: 163, Protein: 9g, Carbs: 14.2g, Fats: 8.9g

42. Chicken Walnut Salad

Ingredients:

6 oz skinless and boneless chicken breast

1 cup baby spinach

1 small tomato, chopped

1 small onion, sliced

1 large cucumber, sliced

2 tbsp minced walnuts

1 tbsp olive oil

Salt to taste

Preparation:

Rinse the chicken under running water and pat-dry with a kitchen paper. Transfer to a cutting board and cut into bite-sized pieces. Set aside.

Preheat the oil in a large skillet over a medium-high heat. Add chicken and cook for 4-5 minutes, or until golden brown. Remove from the heat and set aside to cool completely.

Wash and prepare the remaining vegetables.

In a large salad bowl, combine spinach, tomatoes, onions, and cucumber. Drizzle with lemon juice and top with walnuts.

Serve immediately.

Nutritional information per serving: Kcal: 248, Protein: 23.8g, Carbs: 11.8g, Fats: 13.1 g

43. Tomato Greens Salad

Ingredients:

1 large chopped tomato

1 small sliced onion

1 cup Iceberg lettuce

1 cup chopped spinach

1 cup arugula

1 red bell pepper

1 tbsp avocado oil

1 tbsp apple cider vinegar

½ tsp sea salt

¼ tsp red pepper

Preparation:

In a large colander, combine lettuce, spinach, and arugula. Rinse well under running water and drain. Roughly chop with your hands and transfer to a large salad bowl. Set aside.

Wash the bell pepper and cut lengthwise in half. Remove

the seeds and chop into bite-sized pieces. Set aside.

In a small mixing bowl, combine avocado oil, apple cider vinegar, salt, and pepper. Mix until well combined and set aside.

Now, combine all vegetables in a salad bowl and drizzle with oil. Mix until well incorporated and serve immediately.

Nutritional information per serving: Kcal: 140, Protein: 5.4g, Carbs: 27g, Fats: 2.9g

44. Cheese Salad with Cucumber

Ingredients:

1 cup cottage cheese

2 large cucumbers, sliced

2 large eggs

1 cup Iceberg lettuce

1 tbsp almond oil

¼ tsp dried thyme

¼ tsp dried dill

½ tsp salt

¼ tsp smoked paprika

Preparation:

Wash the cucumbers and cut into small chunks. Sprinkle with some salt and set aside.

Place the eggs in a deep pot and cover with water. Bring to a boil over a medium-high heat. Cook for 10-12 minutes. Remove from the heat and transfer to a separate bowl with ice cold water. After few minutes, gently peel and cut into bite-sized pieces.

In a small mixing bowl, combine almond oil, dried thyme, dried dill, salt, and smoked paprika. Mix until combined and set aside.

Now, add eggs to a bowl with cucumbers and pour over the dressing. Give it a good stir and serve immediately.

Enjoy!

Nutritional information per serving: Kcal: 284, Protein: 24g, Carbs: 16.5g, Fats: 14.4g

45. Green Bean Radish Salad with Spicy Tuna

Ingredients:

½ cup canned green beans

1 large tomato

2 cups shredded radish

1 cup canned tuna

½ tsp chili powder

1 tbsp olive oil

¼ tsp dried thyme

¼ tsp ground cumin

Preparation:

Place the radish in a large colander and rinse well under running water. Drain and transfer to a cutting board. Shred or cut into thin strips and place in a large salad bowl. Set aside.

In a small mixing bowl, combine chili powder, olive oil, dried thyme, and ground cuming. Mix until combined and set aside.

Now, combine radish, chopped tomato, and green beans in

a bowl. Stir once and top with tuna.

Finally, drizzle all with spicy sauce and serve immediately.

Enjoy!

Nutritional information per serving: Kcal: 272, Protein: 25.8g, Carbs: 10g, Fats: 14.7g

46. Egg Onion Salad

Ingredients:

4 large eggs

2 medium-sized onions

1 grated carrot

1 cup spinach

1 tbsp lemon juice

1 tbsp olive oil

¼ tsp ground cumin

¼ tsp dried dill

Salt and pepper to taste

Preparation:

Peel the onions and cut into thin rings. Place in a small bowl and sprinkle with some salt. Let it sit for 10 minutes.

Place the eggs in a deep pot and cover with water. Bring to a boil over a medium-high heat. Cook for 10-12 minutes. When done, remove from the heat and transfer to a bowl with ice cold water. Let it chill for a while and then peel. Cut into bite-sized pieces and set aside.

In a small bowl, combine olive oil, lemon juice, ground cumin, dried dill, salt, and pepper. Mix until well combined and set aside.

Now, in a large salad bowl combine onions, eggs, spinach, and carrot. Drizzle with previously prepared dressing and give it a good stir.

Serve immediately.

Nutritional information per serving: Kcal: 266, Protein: 14.6g, Carbs: 14.9g, Fats: 17.2g

47. Cheese Lettuce Salad

Ingredients:

2 cups Iceberg lettuce

1 cup cottage cheese

2 tbsp canned corn

1 small chili pepper

1 tbsp lime juice

1 tbsp avocado oil

Salt to taste

Preparation:

Using a large colander, rinse the lettuce under running water. Drain and chop into small pieces. Set aside.

Cut the chili pepper in half and remove the seeds. Chop into small pieces and set aside.

In a large bowl, combine lettuce, cottage cheese, corn, and chili pepper. Drizzle with lime juice, avocado oil, and salt. Mix until well combined and serve immediately.

Nutritional information per serving: Kcal: 503, Protein: 41.8g, Carbs: 70.6g, Fats: 10g

48. Couscous Salad with Cucumber and Goat's Cheese

Ingredients:

¼ cup couscous

¼ cup soft goat's cheese

½ sliced cucumber

½ sliced purple onion

1 tbsp finely chopped parsley

1 tsp salt

¼ tsp ground white pepper

¼ tsp dried thyme

¼ tsp turmeric powder

1 tbsp freshly squeezed lemon juice

1 cup reduced-fat Greek yogurt

Preparation:

Place couscous in a small saucepan and pour in 1/3 cup of water. Sprinkle with some salt and optionally with some olive oil. Stir all well and bring to a boil. Reduce the heat to low and cover. Cook until all the liquid has evaporated, stirring occasionally. Remove from the heat and let it sit, covered, for another 10 minutes. Fluff couscous with a fork and set aside.

Heat a large wok pan over medium-high heat and optionally grease with some olive oil. Add onions and briefly cook, for 1-2 minutes.

Now, add couscous and sprinkle with parsley, salt, white pepper, thyme, and turmeric powder. Cook for 4-5 minutes, stirring constantly. Remove from the heat and transfer to a bowl. Add goat's cheese and cucumber. Drizzle with lemon juice and stir all well.

Serve with Greek yogurt.

Nutritional information per serving: Kcal: 459, Protein: 32.8g, Carbs: 53.2g, Fats: 12.9g

49. Asparagus Zucchini Salad

Ingredients:

10oz chopped asparagus

1 medium zucchini

¼ cup sliced radish

¼ cup soft goat's cheese

2 cups chopped baby spinach

2 tbsp drained green peas

1 tbsp pine nuts

1 tsp olive oil

1 tbsp lemon juice

½ tsp salt

Preparation:

Preheat the oven to 425 degrees F. Line a baking sheet with parchment paper and set aside.

Cut off dry ends of the asparagus and rinse well under cold running water. Place on the prepared baking sheet and sprinkle with salt. Optionally, drizzle with some olive oil and roast for 15-20 minutes. Remove from the oven and set aside.

Run zucchini through spiralizer and briefly cook in a wok pan over high heat.

In another bowl, combine the remaining ingredients and add asparagus. Sprinkle with salt, olive oil, and lemon juice.

Serve immediately.

Nutritional information per serving: Kcal: 440, Protein: 26.3g, Carbs: 25.9g, Fats: 24.3g

50. Quinoa Mozzarella Salad with Beans

Ingredients:

1 cup quinoa

2oz sliced mozzarella

½ cup drained green beans

1 chopped tomato

2 cup chopped spinach

1 tsp turmeric powder

½ tsp sea salt

¼ tsp chili powder

¼ tsp cumin powder

Preparation:

Place the quinoa in a heavy-bottomed pot. Add 2 cups of water and bring to a boil. Reduce the heat to low and cook for 12-15 minutes. When done, remove from the heat and set aside to cool. Fluff with a fork and set aside.

Using a large colander, rinse the spinach thoroughly under running water. Drain and chop into small pieces. Place in a large salad bowl, along with chopped tomato and green beans.

Sprinkle all with turmeric powder, sea salt, chili powder, and cumin powder. Add cheese and quinoa. Give it a good stir and serve immediately.

Enjoy!

Nutritional information per serving: Kcal: 437, Protein: 28.2g, Carbs: 52g, Fats: 14.3g

51.   Kale Salad with Tomatoes and Corn

Ingredients:

2 cups chopped kale

¼ cup sliced radishes

½ cup drained corn

1 cup cherry tomatoes

½ cup cottage cheese

1 tbsp vegetable oil

1 tbsp lemon juice

¼ tsp salt

¼ tsp dried marjoram

Preparation:

Rinse kale thoroughly under cold running water and drain in a large colander. Set aside.

Rinse the cherry tomatoes and remove the stems. Cut each into halves and set aside.

Heat a small, non-stick grill pan over medium-high heat and briefly brown corn, for 5-6 minutes, stirring constantly.

Transfer to a bowl and add the remaining ingredients.

Sprinkle with oil, lemon juice, salt, and marjoram.

Serve immediately.

Nutritional information per serving: Kcal: 451, Protein: 26.2g, Carbs: 54.1g, Fats: 17.9g

MEAL RECIPES

1. Flaxseed-Cranberry Bread

This delicious bread recipe is more than an awesome and healthy treat, it is also perfect for a cancer preventive diet thanks to important compounds found in flaxseeds. Flaxseeds have an enormous amount of lignans which block and suppress carcinogenic cells, it is also rich in omega-3 fatty acids (as do walnuts) that are thought to protect against colon, heart and prostate cancer.

Ingredients:

¼ cup Lemon juice

¼ cup Canola oil

½ cup Honey

2 tsp Vanilla

1 cup Almond milk

½ cup Ground flaxseed

2 cups Whole wheat

2 tsp Baking powder

1 tsp Baking soda

¾ cup Dried or frozen cranberries

½ cups Walnuts, chopped

Instructions:

- ✓ Preheat oven to 350°F and oil a loaf pan;
- ✓ In a medium sized bowl whisk together lemon juice, oil, honey, vanilla and almond milk;
- ✓ Add the ground flaxseed and dry ingredients, stir until just combined;
- ✓ Toss the cranberries and walnuts and pour the batter into the prepared pan;
- ✓ Bake for 40 minutes, until golden brown;
- ✓ Let it cool before slicing.

2. Ginger Mackerel & Cucumber Salad

This amazing dish brings out the delicious taste and flavor of this ginger and cucumber combination. Ginger root is a powerful anti-inflammatory and anti-oxidant that acts by reducing the ability of tumors to grow. On the other hand, cucumber has lignans that have been shown to reduce the risk of uterine and prostate cancer.

Ingredients:

2 Mackerel fillets

1 Onion, chopped

1 Red pepper, chopped

1 lemon juice

Fresh ginger, grated

1 garlic clove, minced

3 tbsp honey, separated 1-2

1 cucumber

2 tbsp dried wakame (seaweed)

4 tbsp Rice vinegar

1 tsp Sesame oil

1 tbsp Sesame seeds

Salt and pepper to taste

Instructions:

- ✓ Rub the fish with salt and pepper;
- ✓ Prepare the marinade by mixing lemon juice, ginger and 1 tbsp honey, pour onto the fish and chill for about 30 minutes;
- ✓ Cut the cucumber into thin slices and sprinkle with salt, preserve for 10 minutes;
- ✓ Rehydrate the wakame by soaking in water as package instructions;
- ✓ Prepare the dressing mixing rice vinegar, sesame oil and remaining honey;
- ✓ Meanwhile, heat the grill and punt the fish skin side up on a baking sheet, grill for 5 minutes each side
- ✓ Wash and rinse the cucumber to remove the salt;
- ✓ Toss the cucumber and wakame together and sprinkle with sesame seeds;
- ✓ Serve the mackerel with the cucumber salad and spoon the dressing onto each serving.

3. Stuffed Peppers

With this dish you will enjoy the perks of organic bell peppers, turmeric, garlic, onions and tomatoes, all filth with vitamins and compounds that boost your system and protect your body. For example, turmeric stimulates the apoptosis in cancer and reduces tumor growth, and tomatoes are a high source of Lycopene that also aids preventing growth cell of prostate cancer.

Ingredients:

2 to 3 Colored bell peppers

1 cup Brown rice

1 tsp Cumin

½ tsp Turmeric

3 cups water

Half Eggplant, chopped

1 Zucchini, chopped

1 Red Onion, diced

1 Garlic cloves, smashed

1 cup Natural tomato sauce

3 tbsp Olive oil

Salt and pepper to taste

Instructions:

- ✓ Preheat the oven to 380°F;
- ✓ Prepare de peppers: cut side up and remove seeds, scrub them inside-out with salt and pepper;
- ✓ In a saucepan boiled the water, rice, cumin, turmeric and a dash of salt, for about 12 to 15 minutes;
- ✓ Wash, peel and cut the eggplant, zucchini and onions into dices;
- ✓ In an oiled saucepan stir fry the vegetables until softened;
- ✓ When rice is ready, add it in batches to the vegetables, mixing between batches;
- ✓ Add the tomato sauce and mix well;
- ✓ Spoon filing into the prepared peppers, cover them with foil and bake for 20 minutes;
- ✓ Remove the foil and bake for 3 to 5 more minutes.

4. Raspberry Salad

This refreshing salad aims to care for your health, using the benefits of raspberries which contain ellagic acid, polyphenol and other compounds that promote the elimination of carcinogenic substances and inhibit angiogenesis.

Ingredients:

4 cups Romaine Lettuce, sliced

2 cups Cress

2 cups Radicchio

2 cups Raspberries

¼ cup Almonds, chopped

6 tbsp Natural Pomegranate juice

3 tbsp Olive oil

3 tbsp Apple vinegar

2 tbsp Honey

Salt and pepper to taste

Instructions:

✓ Prepare the vinaigrette by mixing pomegranate juice,

olive oil, apple vinegar, honey, salt and pepper, preserve;
- ✓ Wash and rinse the lettuce, cress and radicchio, cut roughly;
- ✓ In a big bowl put the green mixture and pour the vinaigrette on top and stir until combined;
- ✓ Sprinkle with almonds and serve.

5. Fruity Morning Booster

Breakfast is the most important food of the day, this food will provide the energy to embrace your day full of energy while clean your body and revitalize your health. The incredible properties in these ingredients have shown to slow and prevent cancer development in color, liver, breast and prostate cells.

Ingredients:

1 Ripe bananas, smashed

1 cup Whole wheat

¾ cup Almond milk

1 egg, slightly beaten

1 tsp Baking powder

1 tsp Baking soda

1 tsp Salt

2 tsp Vanilla

¼ cup Walnuts, chopped

Preferred jam, fresh fruits or maple syrup.

1 cup hot water

2 tsp Green tea

1 tsp Ginger, minced

Half lemon juice

Honey to taste

Instructions:

For the tea:

- ✓ Put the tea and ginger into the hot water and set aside while making the pancakes;
- ✓ Then add the lemon juice and honey.

For the pancakes:

- ✓ Blend together almond milk, egg, banana, wheat, baking powder, baking soda, salt and vanilla;
- ✓ Coated a skillet with cooking spray and heat over medium;
- ✓ Pour ¼ cup batter onto the pan and sprinkle with walnuts, cook 1 minute each side;
- ✓ Serve with preferred jam, fresh fruits or maple syrup.

6. Dried Tomatoes Focaccia

This is a healthy meal option and a tasty treat. Keep enjoying the benefits of tomatoes, this time among whole-wheat, which is a great source of fiber. Dietary fiber is related with a lower risk some types of cancer, such as prostate, colon and colorectal cancer.

Ingredients:

¾ lukewarm water

2 tsp dry active yeast

1 tbsp honey

4 tbsp olive oil, divided

1 ½ cups whole wheat

1 tsp kosher salt

1 garlic clove, minced

½ cup dried tomatoes, chopped

1 tsp dried oregano

Instructions:

- ✓ Prepare a baking pan with baking spray;
- ✓ In a bowl combine water, yeast and honey, let it rest for 2 or 3 minutes;

- ✓ Add in the flour, garlic and oil, knead for 5 minutes;
- ✓ Spread the dough in the prepared pan and let it rise for 30 minutes;
- ✓ Once risen, preheat oven to 375°F;
- ✓ Sprinkle kosher salt, dried tomatoes and oregano over the dough and slightly press, drizzle with olive oil and bake for 10 minutes.

7. Funfetti Cabbage Slaw

Red cabbage is rich flavonoids that prevent the growth of precancerous cells that can lead to colon, colorectal and prostate cancer. In addition, carrots are loaded with beta-carotene, which are known for preventing a wide range of cancers, including prostate cancer.

Ingredients:

2 tbsp apple vinegar

1 tsp honey

1 tsp Dijon mustard

1 tsp poppy seeds

1 tsp olive oil

Salt and pepper to taste

1 cup green cabbage, thinly sliced

1 cup red cabbage, thinly sliced

½ cup carrots, shredded

¼ cup brazil nuts, chopped

Instructions:

✓ For the vinaigrette combine vinegar, honey, mustard,

poppy seeds, olive oil, salt and pepper;
- ✓ Prepared the vegetables as described;
- ✓ Pour the vinaigrette onto the vegetables and toss;
- ✓ Sprinkle with Brazil nuts and serve.

8. Healthy Chili

This chili is full of ingredients that are packed with nutrients: turmeric, onions, carrots, peppers, garlic, beans, and tomatoes! Everything in this mouthwatering plate is designed to improve your health. Even the simplest thing like garlic has amazing benefits with many anti-cancer effects. This organosulfur compounds like allicin and alliin triggers cell death in prostate cancer.

Ingredients:

1 tbsp oil

Half onion chopped

2 bay leaves

1 tsp cumin

½ tsp turmeric

2 stalks celery, chopped

1 carrot, peeled and chopped

2 bell peppers, chopped

1 chili pepper, chopped

2 garlic cloves, minced

1 cup kidney beans, cooked and drained

1 cup black beans, cooked and drained

2 tomatoes, cooked, peeled and chopped

1 cup kernel corn

2 tbsp chili powder

Salt to taste

Freshly ground black pepper

Instructions:

- ✓ Prepare the ingredients as described;
- ✓ Heat the oil in a sauce pan and toss onions, bay leaves, cumin, turmeric and salt;
- ✓ Add in celery, peppers and garlic, and simmer for 5 minutes;
- ✓ Mix the tomatoes, chili powder, black pepper and all beans, let it boiled then simmer for 20 minutes;
- ✓ Toss the corn and combine, cook for 5 more minutes;
- ✓ Serve hot.

9. Mighty Broccoli

Among the cruciferous, broccoli is well-known for preventing pre-cancerous cells from developing into malignant tumors; scientific studies demonstrated that it creates a strong defense against lung, prostate, breast, stomach, liver and ovarian cancer.

Ingredients:

Olive oil

2 garlic clove, minced and divided

1 tbsp ginger, minced

4 cups Broccoli florets

1 Onion

2 tbsp honey

1 tbsp apple vinegar

Kosher salt to taste

Fresh ground black pepper to taste

Instructions:

- ✓ Preheat the oven to 400°F, prepare a baking pan coated with olive oil;
- ✓ Combine garlic, broccoli florets and salt, spread in the

baking sheet and bake for 5 minutes
- ✓ Meanwhile, heat a skillet over medium with olive oil and sauté onions and a pinch of salt, until almost cooked;
- ✓ Add in garlic and ginger, stir over;
- ✓ Add honey and vinegar, low the heat;
- ✓ When ready, incorporate the broccoli and stir all together;
- ✓ Serve and enjoy.

10. Veggie Lasagna

This veggie lasagna is the perfect replacement for processed pasta, and it also provides the benefits of mushrooms, which contain polysaccharides and Lentinant, both anti-carcinogenic compounds.

Ingredients:

1 tbsp olive oil

2 garlic cloves, minced

2 cups mushrooms

2 cups baby spinach

1 cup natural tomato sauce

2 to 3 zucchini, thinly sliced

Salt and pepper to taste

Instructions:

- ✓ Preheat the oven to 375°F;
- ✓ Heat the oil in a skillet and add in garlic, mushroom, salt and pepper, cook for a couple minutes;
- ✓ Incorporate baby spinach and tomato sauce, cook for 3 or 4 minutes;
- ✓ In a baking dish spoon some sauce at the bottom and

arrange zucchini slices on top, repeat until all ingredients have been used;
- ✓ Bake for 20 minutes;
- ✓ Let it cool for a few minutes and serve.

11. Savory Papaya Salad

This exotic salad emphasizes the benefits of papayas, a rich fount of vitamin C and folic acid. This fruit has been shown to minimize absorption of cancer-causing nitrosamines from processed foods and prevent certain cancers, such as ovarian and prostate cancer.

Ingredients:

1 garlic cloves, minced

Kosher salt to taste

2 tbsp Wine vinegar

2 tbsp honey

2 tsp sriracha sauce

1 firm papaya, seeded and diced

1 red onion, sliced

1 tsp paprika

Fresh ground black pepper to taste

Instructions:

- ✓ Mix together papaya and onions
- ✓ In a medium bowl combine garlic, salt, vinegar, honey, sriracha sauce, paprika and ground pepper;

- ✓ Pour the mixture onto the papayas and onions and toss to incorporate;
- ✓ Serve and enjoy.

12. Veggie Curry

Prepare to be pampered, with this veggie curry. You will absorb all the vitamins that you should to fight cancer. It will provide you with lots of lignans, flavonoids, beta-carotenes, lycopene, and more compounds that promise to take your health to another level and prevent you from getting a wide range of diseases.

Ingredients:

Half onion, chopped

2 garlic cloves, smashed

1 tbsp ginger, grated

¼ dried tomatoes, chopped

1 tbsp olive oil

1 tsp cumin

½ tsp turmeric

½ tsp coriander

2 tbsp lentils

3 tbsp coconut milk

1 tbsp ground flaxseed

½ cup garbanzo beans, cooked and drained

½ cup pureed pumpkin

Salt and pepper to taste

Fresh coriander for sprinkle

Instructions:

- ✓ Blend together onion, garlic, ginger, pumpkin and tomatoes until it resembles a puree.
- ✓ Heat oil in a saucepan and add in cumin, turmeric and coriander, then incorporate the puree mixture and let it boil;
- ✓ Lower the heat and add lentils and coconut cream, simmer for 5 minutes;
- ✓ Stir garbanzo beans and flaxseed and cook for 3 to 5 more minutes;
- ✓ Serve and sprinkle with fresh coriander.

13. Saucy Soup

This saucy soup represents a new way to taste and harness the qualities of pumpkin and apples. On one hand, pumpkins are rich in carotenoids, lycopene and lutein, that increase the growth of immune cells and their capacity to attack tumor cells; on the other hand, apples are a good source of antioxidants and flavonoids.

Ingredients:

3 cups pureed pumpkin

2 large red apples

2 tbsp olive oil

2 cups chicken broth

½ tsp cinnamon

Salt and pepper to taste

¼ chopped brazil nuts, for sprinkle

Instructions:

- ✓ In a skillet, heat oil and stir-fry diced apples with cinnamon, until apples start to caramelize;
- ✓ Incorporate pumpkin puree, then chicken broth, salt and pepper, cook for 7 minutes;

- ✓ Let it cool for a few minutes and blend together;
- ✓ Heat again if desired;
- ✓ Serve with Brazilian nuts sprinkled on top.

14.   Green Tea Avocado Ice-Cream

This ice-cream it's full of vitamins, starting with an avocado base that is highly rich in antioxidants, aiding your system to attack free radicals. This innovative way of eating avocado by mixing it with matcha (a Japanese green tea powder) is definitely an enhanced way to enjoy ice cream.

Ingredients:

2 avocados, peeled and frozen

½ cup almond milk

½ cup coconut milk

2 tbsp matcha powder

¼ cup dates, chopped

Dash ground cardamom

Instructions:

- ✓ Blend together almond milk, coconut milk, dates, cardamom and matcha powder, *add 1 to 2 tbsp honey if desired;
- ✓ Gradually incorporate frozen avocado until reached a creamy texture;
- ✓ Serve immediately or freeze overnight.

15. Matcha Muffin Delight

We've been talking about the benefits of green tea, matcha is an incredible form of green tea powder. To enjoy its benefits let's use it in dishes for creating healthy desserts like this one. This Japanese green tea powder is the richest source of polyphenols and catechins that are known for inhibiting metastases. Also, dark chocolate chips bring out the real flavor while providing a great source of antioxidants.

Ingredients:

2/3 almond milk

2 tbsp cider vinegar

1 tbsp ground flaxseed

3 tbsp canola oil

1/3 honey

Half banana, smashed

1 ½ whole wheat flour

2 tsp baking powder

½ tsp salt

2 tbsp matcha powder

Dark chocolate chips *>70% cocoa

Instructions:

- ✓ Preheat the oven to 375°F and prepare a muffin pan;
- ✓ Combine almond milk, vinegar, and flaxseed, set aside for 5 minutes;
- ✓ Mix in oil, honey and banana;
- ✓ In a large bowl, combine flour, baking powder, salt and matcha powder;
- ✓ Pour liquid mixture into flour mixture and mix until almost combined (do not overmix);
- ✓ Add chocolate chips and slightly stir;
- ✓ Fill ¾ of the muffin pan with batter and bake for about 15 to 18 minutes.

16.　Green Stuffed Mushrooms

In this plate we combined the powerful properties of mushrooms, garlic, spinach, bell pepper and onion, but also we incorporated seaweed (wakame), which contain molecules that slow cancer growth in breast, colon and prostate cancers.

Ingredients:

2 large Portobello mushrooms caps

2 tbsp olive oil, divided

1 garlic clove

1 cup baby spinach

1 cup green bell pepper, diced

1 small onion, diced

½ dried wakame

1 to 2 tbsp oyster sauce

Salt and pepper to taste

Sesame seeds for sprinkle

Instructions:

- ✓ Preheat oven to 400°F, slightly grease a baking pan;

- ✓ Rehydrate wakame as package instructions;
- ✓ In a large skillet heat the oil and stir fry bell pepper and onions until almost tender;
- ✓ Add spinach and garlic, sauté for a minute, and pour the oyster sauce, salt and pepper, cook for 3 to 4 more minutes;
- ✓ Remove from fire, stir rinsed wakame;
- ✓ Serve and sprinkle with sesame seeds.

17. Sauteed Shrimp & Wheat-Berry

Besides all the well-known benefits provided by broccoli, garlic, onion, scallions and endives, this recipe calls for wheat-berry, which contain wheat germ, thiamine, folate, zinc, and more compounds that ensure a balanced diet to prevent your system from any kind of disease.

Ingredients:

1 cup wheat berry

4 tbsp water

2 tbsp honey

2 tbsp rice vinegar

2 garlic clove, minced

2 cups broccoli florets

1 red onion, sliced

1 scallions, sliced

1 Belgian endive, sliced

2 cups raw shrimps

2 tbsp olive oil

Salt and pepper to taste

Instructions:

- ✓ Cook wheat berry as package instructions say, drain and let it cool;
- ✓ Meanwhile, whisk together water, honey, vinegar and garlic;
- ✓ Heat a skillet oiled and sauté the drained wheat-berry over high heat, stir constantly until crispy, preserve in a bowl;
- ✓ In the same skillet, sauté broccoli for a couple of minutes, add in onions and endives, salt and pepper, cook for 5 minutes;
- ✓ Incorporate shrimps and cook, add the wet mixture and stir for 2 minutes;
- ✓ Return wheat berry and toss until everything's combine;
- ✓ Serve and sprinkle with scallions.

18. Mix Quinoa Salad

The meal has a lot of phytochemicals, lycopene, lignans and allicin that not only prevent your system from diseases, but help to fight any carcinogenic cells, inhibiting them from spreading around our body. This dish also uses quinoa to provide a great amount of soluble fibers.

Ingredients:

¾ cup uncooked quinoa

1 cup natural chicken broth

½ cup dried tomatoes, chopped

1 garlic clove, smashed

2 cups kale

2 cups red cabbage

1 avocado, peeled, pitted and chopped

1 tbsp olive oil

1 tbsp balsamic vinegar

3 tbsp brazil nuts, chopped

Salt and pepper to taste

Instructions:

- ✓ Boil the broth and add in quinoa, salt and pepper, let it cook for 10 minutes, until the quinoa is tender and liquid is absorbed;
- ✓ In an oiled skillet quickly sauté garlic, kale, cabbage, salt and pepper, over high heat constantly stirring;
- ✓ Stir in quinoa and dried tomatoes, combine;
- ✓ Serve with avocados on top and drizzle with balsamic vinegar.

19.   Green Soup Kick

Fully charge your system with this green soup, with vegetables packed with beta-carotene, glutathione, vitamins, and many antioxidants that will increase the production of protective enzymes that inhibit angiogenesis. Also, brazil nuts contain a lot of selenium, which has been linked with prostate cancer treatments.

Ingredients:

Half leek, sliced

1 garlic clove, minced

2 cups broccoli florets

2 cups asparagus, chopped

1 cup peas

5 cups natural vegetable or chicken broth

1 to 2 tsp sriracha sauce

Half lemon juice

Salt and fresh ground pepper to taste

Chopped brazil nuts for sprinkle

Instructions:

- ✓ Heat an oiled skillet and sauté leeks for 5 minutes, toss garlic and cook for one more minute;
- ✓ Add broth, broccoli florets, asparagus and peas, let it simmer for 7 minutes;
- ✓ Blend the soup and season with sriracha, lemon, salt and pepper;
- ✓ Serve and sprinkle with chopped brazil nuts.

20. Fruity Bars

Satisfy your cravings with these healthy fruity & nutty bars, rich in omega-3 fatty acids and many anti-carcinogenic agents found in peaches. On the other hand, pineapples are full of bromelain, an important component that fights cancer even better than the regular chemo drugs.

Ingredients:

1 ½ cup almond flour

1 ½ cup oat flour

½ cup honey

2 tbsp canola oil

3 cups peaches, chopped

1 cup nectarines, chopped

1 cups pineapples, chopped

1 cups cherries

½ cup orange juice

½ cup pomegranate juice

2 tsp granulated jelly

Instructions:

- ✓ Preheat the oven to 400°F and slightly grease a baking pan;
- ✓ Blend together almond flour, oat flour, honey and canola, until form clumps;
- ✓ Pour the mixture in to the baking pan and press down to form a layer, bake for 10 minutes or until golden brown;
- ✓ Meanwhile, prepare the filling heating an oiled saucepan to medium heat, stir in all the fruits and juice and simmer for 5 minutes;
- ✓ Mix the jelly with cold water;
- ✓ Remove the filling and cool for 5 minutes, incorporate hydrated jelly and stir until well combine;
- ✓ Pour the filling onto the baked crust and freeze over night;
- ✓ Cut the pie into bars and enjoy.

21. Best-Healthy Tomato Sauce

We bring the ultimate healthy tomato sauce to boost your body with the goodness of lycopene in tomatoes. This recipe is packed with different vegetables that provide a high source of fiber. Mixing them together is the best way to get the most from all the nutrients in them.

Ingredients:

3 tbsp Olive oil

3 cloves Garlic, minced

1 large Onion, diced

1 large Carrots, diced

1 Green pepper, diced

1 Zucchini, diced

1 cup Natural Chicken broth

2 pounds Tomatoes

2 tsp Paprika

3 tsp dried Oregano

3 dried Bay leaves

3 dried Basil leaves

Salt and pepper to taste

Instructions:

- ✓ In a large saucepan heat oil and add paprika, oregano bay and basil leaves, stir for less than a minute and incorporate carrots and peppers, cook for 3 minutes and toss onions, garlic and zucchini, salt and pepper, cook for 8 to 10 minutes, after this, using tongs remove bay and basil leaves;
- ✓ Meanwhile, in another saucepan bring water to boil and add the tomatoes for 5 to 7 minutes, until the peel starts to rip, remove from heat and add cold water. When cold, finish peeling the tomatoes and drain the remaining water;
- ✓ When peeled, blend the tomatoes with chicken broth and pour into the vegetables, let it simmer for 20 minutes, stirring occasionally;
- ✓ If desired, you can blend all the ingredients to have an homogenic sauce, and add one or two anchovies' fillets to make the perfect sauce for a pizza.

22. No-Knead Whole Wheat Pizza Dough

Did you know there's a way to enjoy pizza and at the same time eat healthy? Because we all love to eat pizza, we want to show you a healthy pizza dough that can perfectly replace the processed pizza store. For enhanced taste and results, coat it with all natural tomato sauce, almond cheese (or other low fat cheese) and your favorite toppings.

Ingredients:

3 cups whole wheat flour

1 tbsp instant dry yeast

1 tsp kosher salt

1 cup lukewarm water

1 tbsp olive oil

1 tbsp honey

Instructions:

- ✓ In a large bowl combine dry ingredients;
- ✓ In a small bowl combine wet ingredients and pour it into the flour whilst stirring until incorporate and a shaggy dough forms;
- ✓ Transfer the dough into a clean and grease bowl and

cover with plastic wrap, let it rest for 1 hour or until double it sizes;
- ✓ Gently deflate the dough using a wooden spoon, make two or three folders and let rest for 30 more minutes;
- ✓ When dough's ready, use a rolling pin to create a thin layer and cover with your favorites ingredients.
- ✓ Bake at 450°F for 10 to 13 minutes.

23. Raspberry Crumbles

This decadent dessert has an incredible taste perfect to satisfy any craving for sweets, and also provides a high amount of nutrients and compounds beneficial towards the prevention of cancer. Such is the case of the ellagic acid found in raspberries, which stimulates apoptosis, being a natural anti-carcinogenic and anti-mutagen fruit.

Ingredients:

2 cups raspberries

2 tbsp honey, divided

3 tbsp whole-wheat flour, divided

1 tbsp pomegranate juice

½ rolled oats

¼ cup chopped almonds

½ tsp cinnamon

1 tbsp canola oil

Instructions:

- ✓ Preheat oven to 400°F;
- ✓ Combine raspberries, 1 tbsp honey, pomegranate juice and 1 tbsp flour, divided among 4 ramekins;

- ✓ Combine oats, almonds, cinnamon, remaining honey and flour, add oil and stir until just combine. Sprinkle over the fruit mix;
- ✓ Bake for 20 minutes, let it cool for 15 minutes before serving.

24. Mini Calzone

We want to teach you that been healthy doesn't mean you can't eat delicious food, so we bring this awesome mini calzone, a perfect treat for a family dinner while you stay on your nutritious diet.

Ingredients:

1 ball homemade "No-Knead Whole-Wheat Pizza Dough"

1 cup Tomato sauce

½ cup Almond cheese

½ cup Fresh basil

1 cup Baby spinach

Half Red onion

¼ cup Black olives

1 tsp Dried Oregano

1 tsp Dried Garlic

1 tsp Dried Thyme

1 tsp Red pepper flakes

½ tsp Ground black pepper

2 tbsp Olive oil

1 egg

Instructions:

- ✓ Preheat oven to 400°F
- ✓ Cut the dough into 4 pieces, spread the pieces evenly in a floured surface to form 4 small pizzas;
- ✓ Toss all the filling ingredients together until combine;
- ✓ Spoon one or two tablespoon of filling mix on one half of each pizza and gently fold to form a half moon shape;
- ✓ Press the edges to seal;
- ✓ Coat with a beaten egg and sprinkle some kosher salt;
- ✓ Bake for 18 minutes.

25. Tuna Healthy-Patties

For this plate we are focusing on the goodness of omega-3 fatty acids contained in tuna fillets, the anti-inflammatory and antioxidant properties of ginger, as well as olive oil, that provides more antioxidants and vitamins for your daily life.

Ingredients:

2 Tuna fillets, skinless

1 tbsp Curry paste

1 tbsp fresh ginger, grated

1 tbsp fresh dill, minced

1 tbsp fresh coriander, minced

1 tsp olive oil

Salt and pepper to taste

Ingredients:

- ✓ In a food processor, blend tuna fillets, curry paste, ginger, dill, coriander, salt and pepper;
- ✓ Pour the mix into a bowl and shape into a burger;
- ✓ In an oiled skillet, fry the burgers for 4 minutes each side.

- ✓ Serve with whole wheat bread and preferred salad.

26. Sweet & Spicy Salmon Sunset

In this plate we combine sweetness and spiciness from mango and jalapeños, mangos are full of vitamins and beta-carotene compounds, while jalapeños are high in capsaicin that neutralize substance that might cause cancer.

Ingredients:

2 Salmon fillets

1 big mango, peeled and diced

1 red jalapeño, seeded and minced

1 fresh lemongrass, minced

1 tbsp rice vinegar

1 tbsp honey

2 tbsp olive oil, divided

Salt and pepper to taste

Ingredients:

- ✓ Rub the fillets with salt and pepper;
- ✓ Combine mango, jalapeño, lemongrass, vinegar and honey;
- ✓ In a skillet heat 1 tablespoon of oil, place the salmon and cook for 3 minutes each side, set aside;

- ✓ In the same skillet heat the remaining oil and stir fry the mango mix for 3 or 4 minutes, add in the salmon and coat with juices and fruits;
- ✓ Remove from heat and serve.

27. Fig Salad

Figs are awesome fruits for preventing and fighting cancer. Thanks to its derivatives of benzaldehyde, figs have been demonstrated to shrink tumors, and is also a great bacteria-killer.

Ingredients:

4 figs, chopped

4 cups Romaine lettuce, chopped

½ Basil leaves

¼ Pecans, chopped

3 tbsp Cider vinegar

2 tbsp Fig relish

1 tbsp Olive oil

Salt and pepper to taste

Instructions:

- ✓ In a small bowl whisk together vinegar, relish, oil, salt and pepper;
- ✓ Toss the remaining ingredients in a large bowl;
- ✓ Pour dressing onto the green salad and combine;

- ✓ Serve with one piece of fig on top and sprinkle more chopped pecans.

28. Colorful Skewers

Skewers represent a fun way of cooking and eating, and in this case these colorful skewers are filled with vitamins and beta-carotene found in bell peppers. Also it provides the benefits of bromelain from the pineapple, as mentioned before, this potent compound fights cancer and is more effective than chemo drugs.

Ingredients:

1 Red pepper, chopped

1 Green pepper, chopped

1 Yellow pepper, chopped

1 Red onions, chopped

2 cups chopped Pineapples

2 tbsp Olive oil

1 Lemon juice

2 Garlic cloves, minced

1 tsp Paprika

Salt and pepper to taste

Instructions:

- ✓ Prepare all ingredients as described and thread them into the skewers alternating the ingredients;
- ✓ Whisk together lemon, garlic, paprika, oil, salt and pepper;
- ✓ Coat the skewers with the marinade and let them marinate for 30 minutes;
- ✓ Grill for 10 to 15 minutes.

29.   Easy Garlic Soup

As mentioned before, the anti-cancer benefits of garlic are many. Its immune-enhancing compounds aid the organism to fight and block carcinogenic cells, and studies have linked garlic to lower risk of stomach, colon and prostate cancer.

Ingredients:

6 tbsp Olive oil

1 garlic head

2 tbsp whole-wheat flour

4 cups natural chicken broth

Dried Thyme

Dried Oregano

Dried Basil

Salt and pepper to taste

Instructions:

- ✓ Cut garlic head in half -do not peel-;
- ✓ Heat an oiled saucepan to medium-low heat and place each half head flat, cook until garlic is soft and nicely browned, the peel will come out easily then;

- ✓ Remove from heat and smash the garlic with the flour combining well until a shaggy paste forms;
- ✓ Return to heat and add the hot broth, add thyme, oregano, basil, salt and pepper, cook until reached the desired consistency.

30. Tuna Salad

Once again we want to use the benefits of tuna and its omega-3 fatty acids, but this time combining the properties of radish, which are high in anthocyanins which are powerful anti-cancer molecules that prevent carcinogenic cells from developing.

Ingredients:

2 tune fillet, stir-fry

1 Red pepper

1 Red onion

2 Tomatoes

3 cups romaine lettuce

2 cups radicchio

1 cup radish, sliced

3 tbsp Greek Yoghurt

1 Lemon juice

2 tbsp Olive oil

½ tsp Mustard seeds, grounded

Salt and pepper to taste

Instructions:

- ✓ Whisk together yoghurt, oil, lemon, mustard seeds, salt and pepper;
- ✓ In a large bowl, combine peppers, onions, tomato, lettuce, radicchio and radish;
- ✓ Shred the tuna and stir it into the salad mixture;
- ✓ Drizzle with dressing and toss to incorporate.

31. Basil Arugula Pesto

With this pesto you can create an awesome and healthy pizza or pasta, thanks to the essential oils in basil, which are part of the terpene family. They can promote apoptosis and reduce the spread of carcinogenic-cells.

Ingredients:

4 cups fresh basil

1 ½ cup fresh arugula

3 garlic cloves

½ brazil nuts

Half lemon juice

¼ tsp lemon zest

4 tbsp chicken broth

¼ cup olive oil

Salt and pepper to taste

Instructions:

- ✓ Pour all ingredients into a blender and blend until well mixed.

32. Healthy Sandwich

Alkaline foods such as alfalfa and avocado keep blood ph in its ideal range, which is very important for the prevention and treatment of cancer.

Ingredients:

4 slices Whole-wheat nutty bread

200gr Smoked salmon

1 cup Alfalfa

1 cup Watercress

1 Avocado, smashed

3 tbsp Greek yoghurt

2 tbsp Olive oil

Salt and pepper

Instructions:

- ✓ Smash avocado and mix in yoghurt, oil, salt and pepper;
- ✓ Coat bread slices with avocado mixture;
- ✓ Arrange salmon, alfalfa and watercress, and cover with bread.

ADDITIONAL TITLES FROM THIS AUTHOR

70 Effective Meal Recipes to Prevent and Solve Being Overweight: Burn Fat Fast by Using Proper Dieting and Smart Nutrition

By

Joe Correa CSN

48 Acne Solving Meal Recipes: The Fast and Natural Path to Fixing Your Acne Problems in Less Than 10 Days!

By

Joe Correa CSN

41 Alzheimer's Preventing Meal Recipes: Reduce or Eliminate Your Alzheimer's Condition in 30 Days or Less!

By

Joe Correa CSN

70 Effective Breast Cancer Meal Recipes: Prevent and Fight Breast Cancer with Smart Nutrition and Powerful Foods

By

Joe Correa CSN

www.ingramcontent.com/pod-product-compliance
Lightning Source LLC
Chambersburg PA
CBHW052015070526
44584CB00016B/1766